A GUIDE BOOK OF POLITICAL THEORY

FOR B.A. 1ST SEMESTER STUDENTS OF BODOLAND UNIVERSITY

RITURAJ BASUMATARY

Contents

A Guide Book Of Political Theory

RITURAJ BASUMATARY
M.A.
NET
SLET
MPHIL
ASSISTANT PROFESSOR
BOROBAZAR COLLEGE

BODOLAND UNIVERSITY

B. A. FIRST SEMESTER (REGULAR) CBCS
POLITICAL SCIENCE

DSC-1 A: POLITICAL THEORY

Course Objective: This course aims to introduce certain key aspects of conceptual analysis in political theory and the skills required to engage in debates surrounding the application of the concepts.

1. a. What is Politics?

   b. What is Political Theory and what is its relevance?

2. Concepts: Democracy, Liberty, Equality, Justice, Rights, Gender, Citizenship, Civil Society and State

3. Debates in Political Theory:

   a. Is democracy compatible with economic growth?

   b. On what grounds is censorship justified and what are its limits?

   c. Does protective discrimination violate principles of fairness?

   d. Should the State intervene in the institution of the family?

CHAPTER ONE

INTRODUCING POLITICAL THEORY

What is Politics

Aristotle, the father of Political Science, first made use of the term 'Politics' for his treatise on the state. The term 'Politics' is derived from the Latin word 'Politicus' which in turn is derived from the Greek word 'Polis'. In Greek 'Polis' means city state and the subject that studies its activities is Politics.

The Greeks were the first to conduct a systematic study of Political Science. The Sophists were the first expounders of Political Theory. Later on, Socrates, Plato and Aristotle conducted scientific investigation into the various problems of the state.

The Greeks lived in City States and they made no distinction between a city and a state. We live in large territorial states today, but the Greek meaning can be extended to the study of the modern state also. 'Politics' today is known by the new nomenclature of 'Political Science'. The term 'Political Science' (Science Politique) was coined by the French writer Jean Bodin in the sixteenth century. Political Science is a Social Science systematically dealing with the various problems of the State and the Government.

In other words, Politics generally means struggle for power. Whatever may be the ultimate aim of Politics, but its immediate aim is always power. For example Indian National Congress (INC) vs. Bharatiya Janata Party (BJP) are the example of National Politics in our country.

Political Theory: Meaning and Definition

Before analyzing the definitions of Political Theory as given by some Political Scientists, let us understand the meaning of the two words: 'Political' and 'Theory'.

A. Political

The word 'Political' is the adjective of 'Politics'. In a traditional sense, it means relating to polis i.e. state and government. However in contemporary times, the term 'Political' is defined in a broader way. It means power and power relations. Political relations involve power to a significant extent. Lasswell and Kaplan define Politics as the study of "the shaping and sharing of power".

B. Theory

Theory can be defined as a set of interrelated propositions/ principles/concepts which are designed to explain and synthesise the ideas and conclusions or generalizations pertaining to a discipline. In its traditional form, theory is a normative exercise. It explains and prescribes values and offers a philosophy of the concerned subject. In its modern form, theory is taken to mean a set of tested and valid generalizations arrived at through the use of scientific method of study. It is conceptualized as scientific theory. Several modern scholars however, accept both these forms of theory i.e. normative theory and empirical scientific theory.

Definitions of Political Theory

"Political Theory includes political science and political philosophy". – George Catlin

"A combination of disinterested search for the principles of good state and good society on the one hand and a search for knowledge of political and social reality on the other". – Andrew Hacker

"In a very broad sense political theory is anything about politics or relevant to politics. However, in its specific and narrow sense, it is the disciplined investigation of political problems."

Features/Nature/Characteristics of Political Theory

We can identify the following features or nature or characteristics of Political Theory:-

Political Theory is Theory of Politics which seeks to understand, analyse and explain the phenomena of politics.

1. Political Theory attempts to reform by rectifying the shortcomings in the political life of society.
2. Political Theory, like an ideology also includes a set of beliefs, values and ideas, which stand accepted by the people in the process of their governance.
3. Political Theory involves a systematic reflections on politics or state or government or political institutions.
4. Political Theory is generally the intellectual and moral creation of a single thinker who offers a theoretical explanation of the political reality – the phenomena of state.
5. Political Theory can be normative or empirical or both.
6. Description, analysis, explanation, prediction and change are the goals of Political Theory.
7. Scope of Political Theory covers all areas of political relations.
8. Political Theory is the handiwork of philosophers, historian, economists, theologians, sociologist, thinkers, journalists, intellectuals and all others who try to comprehend and explain the political reality.
9. Finally, Political Theory is related to the state, government and political institutions.

Scope of Political Theory

Political Theory stands for history of political ideas. The earlier political thinkers devoted mainly on the point of distinction between 'state' and 'government'. They regarded 'state' as a collectivity for the sake of promoting some common purpose, and 'government' as its instrument for implementing the will of the community. Till the first half of the 19th century, Political Theory was concerned with the study of 'state' and 'government'. Political Theory as understood in modern times devotes to the study of power. It deals with all those activities connected with the 'struggle for power'.

The modern political scientists point out distinction between 'government' and 'politics'. The basic area of the earlier thinker's concern were the institutional frameworks of the rule of the states like the structure and procedure of the legislative and executive bodies, local self government, political parties, voting etc. which are responsible for the conduct of government.

Political Theory is therefore not only concerned with the study of 'state' and 'government' as conceived till the mid 20th century; it is also presently understood as the study of 'power'. It covers all those activities that are connected with 'power' and the 'struggle for power'.

Importance of Political Theory

Political Theory is useful for us as it helps in understanding the meaning of political concepts by looking at the way they are understood and used in ordinary language.

Political theories debate and examine the various meanings and opinions from different contexts in a systematic manner.

The four ways in which the political theory can be useful to us are:

It helps in understanding how constitutions are shaped in a certain manner, how governments and social lives are arranged in a certain systematic manner by studying and understanding the ideas and principles that are at their base.

It shows the significance of various principles such as rule of law, separation of power, judicial review etc.

Political theory helps bureaucrats, politicians, government officers and advocates to interpret the laws and constitution. It also helps in understanding the problems of society and explore the ways to solve them.

Political theory encourages individuals to examine their ideas and feelings about political things so that they can become moderate in their ideas and feelings.

Different Views of Politics

Marxism

Marxism refers to the political and economic theories brought out by Karl Marx, especially with regard to the capitalistic social structure. Marx analyzed the social structure based on the economic activities and according to him, economy is one of the main requirements for humans to satisfy their needs. There are economic organizations that have been formed in such a way that they decide the social relations, ideologies, political and legal systems between social classes. The forces of production may have unequal relationships and profit sharing, which will lead them to the class struggle. The result of the class struggle will be the Socialism, which is said to have a cooperative ownership in production. However, later on, this Socialism will pave the way to Communism that is the ideal social structure in Marx's point of view and there will neither be social classes nor states but the common ownership of the means of production. This is the simplest idea of Marxism and this theory has been applied in so many other subjects as well. However, it is said that there is no single definitive theory of Marxism.

Liberalism

Liberalism can be identified as a political philosophy that emphasizes the idea of being free and liberate. This idea of being free could be applied to many concepts and situations, but liberalists focus more on democracy, civil rights, property ownership, religion, etc., in general. It was during the period of Enlightenment that this philosophy of Liberalism came into the field. The philosopher called John Locke is said to have introduced this concept. Liberalists rejected the absolute monarchy, the state religion, and the immense power and authority of kings, etc. Instead of the monarchy, liberalists promoted democracy. However, Liberalism gained much attention after the French Revolution and today it is a powerful influencing political force throughout the world.

Marxism vs Liberalism

The difference between Marxism and Liberalism stems from the key idea around which each of these concepts are built. Both Marxism and Liberalism are concepts that are espoused by people all over the world. Marxism was introduced by Karl Marx to explain the changes and developments in the society as a result of the conflict between the elites and the working class people. Liberalism, on the other hand, emphasizes the idea of being free and equal with regard to certain concepts like religion, trade, political freedom, civil rights, etc. Marxism focuses more on establishing a classless society that is called the "Communism" and Liberalism is just a movement that stresses the freedom in behavior or attitudes of individuals. Let us look at these two ideologies; namely, Marxism and Liberalism, and the difference between them in detail.

When we look at both these concepts, we can identify some similarities. Both have relationships with economic, political, and social aspects of a particular society. Both deal with the state of human beings living in the society.

• When we look at differences, we can see that Marxism is a theory whereas Liberalism is an ideology.

• Marxism talks of a social transition and in contrast Liberalism deals with the individual state of being.

However, both theses are very popular in the modern world and they are upheld by many communities around the world.

Communitarian View

According to the communitarian view, the essence of human nature lies in the spirit of cooperation, not conflict. Hence mutual aid and cooperation is the foundation of political organisation. Communitarian sees no basic conflict between the interests of different members of society.

Historical Development of Political Theory

Classical Political Theory:

What we call political theory today is not the product of any particular period or the by-product of research of any single person or few persons. Rather there is a history of development behind which lies the work and research as well as philosophy of numerous persons.

Political scientists and researchers have felt that the political theory can be divided into few stages and some of these are classical political theory, traditional political theory, and modern political theory and post modern political theory. It is to be noted here that this classification is not final. Many political scientists do not agree with this classification. But for clarity of thought and convenience of analysis this classification may be followed.

One aspect of classical political theory is it was dominated by certain eternal values and philosophy. This is specifically to be found in the writings of Plato, Aristotle and some others. Both the Greek philosophers thought of establishing ideal state though the modus operandi of both of them was not same.

But there is a resemblance between the ideal states of Plato and Aristotle. To Plato the mechanism of setting up an ideal state was to entrust a philosopher king with the task of administration of the ideal state because it was believed that he would be able to keep himself above narrow interests and ensure communism of wife, children and property.

Plato believed that in an ideal state there shall be uniformity in education, mode of living etc. But his disciple Aristotle did not give any importance to uniformity. He relied upon the abolition of different forms of inequalities and he arrived at the conclusion that only in polity there can exist such an arrangement.

Both Plato and Aristotle were enamoured by the concepts of good and noble life and they thought that eternal values, goodness and nobleness of life can be realised only through the state and for that reason they were thinking of an ideal state.

Only through unconditional surrender to the authority of ideal state an individual can build up his goodness and nobleness of character. Thus, in the thought system of Plato and Aristotle ethics, philosophy, morality, eternal values etc. were completely mixed together.

In the writings of Plato and Aristotle and many others rationality had a very crucial role to play. Since men are rational they are not supposed to disobey the diktat of eternal values, morality and idealism. Throughout the middle Ages there was a long standing and damaging conflict between the church and the state and the central theme of this conflict was state and politics should be controlled by church and religion.

Some medieval thinkers such as St. Augustine (354-430), St. Thomas Aquinas (1227- 1274) and Marsilius of Padua (1270-1340) were all religious-minded and honest persons. All of them thought of state and politics in the light of religion and honesty. So the classical political theory was shrouded with morality, ethics, religious conceptions and many subjective notions.

Natural Law and Classical Political Theory:

Not only morality, ethics and eternal values managed a vintage position in the classical political theory, concept of natural law earned abundant prominence, wide publicity and approval of large number of philosophers in this stage of political theory. We have already noted that both Plato and Aristotle were profusely influenced by rationalism. Natural law had also a great impact upon their political thought and general ideas.

A large number of thinkers believed that the natural law was the greatest manifestation of reason, rationality, correctness and human intellect. Rational knowledge, goodness, reasonability, justice, structured reality and morality are all embedded in natural law. Politicians, statesmen, philosophers and even a large number of educated people were inclined to give maximum importance to natural law.

In the whole period of classical political theory people were reluctant to give any credence to man-made laws, natural law was the real guiding force of all activities and particularly the political activities of state and men.

The exponents of the classical political theory were so much imbued with the thought and importance of natural law that they started to think both natural law and rationalism as the two sides of the same coin and here the coin is society and its political structure.

The influence of natural law was so much prominent in earlier periods that Christian thinkers and philosophers could not come out of its influence. We know that both Hobbes and Locke paid a good deal of attention to the concept of natural law. They wanted to build up a civil society through the instrumentality of contract.

But even the society made by contract could not get rid of the overwhelming influence of natural law. Many thinkers wanted to build up future society upon the natural law and in their thought and attempt utopianism played the most vital role. They thought of a golden age and good society the basis of which would be natural law. In Rousseau's political thought we find a very fine combination of Plato's idealism, morality and natural law.

Rousseau thought that only the revival of state of nature and that is through the system of contract an ideal society could be built up. Even Marx was not free from the influence of natural law. He tells us that in ancient society there was no discrimination among men and also no exploitation. Everything was managed by law of nature.

The emergence of private property which is an innovation of some men heavily told upon the efficacy of natural law. Natural law was replaced by man made laws and this precipitated the exploitation and degradation of society. Hence we see that classical political theory was dominated by idealism, ethics and natural law.

Modern Traditional Political Theory:

It is very difficult to say assertively when the appearance of modern political theory actually took place and subsequently to thrive but there is an almost agreement in this regard that after Machiavelli (1469-1527) the political theory began to assume a different shape because of the fact that he was the first thinker who strongly advocated for forging a separation between politics and religion.

This attempt of Machiavelli initiated a new trend in political theory and it is politics or political theory has a separate existence and both must maintain separate identity. Machiavelli performed a good job by assertively advocating the divorce between religion and politics. But in spite of this after Machiavelli political theory could not assert itself. Religion clandestinely and sometimes overtly began to influence political theory.

He was thus a political thinker of transition period. West European society was not completely free from the influence of religion. In the political thought of Christian thinkers religion had an important part to play. That is why post-Machiavellian political theory was both modern and traditional.

Modern in the sense that the tremendous influence of church and religion on politics and functions of state that existed in the Middle Ages began to recede. But religion was still a force to reckon with. Hence post-classical political theory is sometimes called modern traditional political theory.

The State as a Machine:

The important characteristic feature of political theory of the modern traditional period is that the state is a machine. In the classical period the state was also considered as a vehicle through which men can realise their noble aspirations. But this role of state could not earn widespread approval from wider sections of society because people were not profoundly interested in ethical, moral and ideological values.

The two exponents of contract theory—Hobbes and Locke—introduced a new thought and vision and it is that the state is a machine through which individuals can achieve certain ends which are associated with their ground to earth life and existence.

According to Hobbes these are peace and security and according to Locke the chief objectives of any political organisation (Locke also uses the term civil society) to ascertain life and liberty and to make proper arrangements for the protection of private property. The political theory adumbrated by Locke unfolded a new concept and it is liberalism. Liberalism is a very complex concept that embraces so many ideas and views and in fact modern traditional theory revolves around this particular concept.

On the other hand, Hobbes gave very little attention to the protection of property and realisation of liberty. To him security and peace were of utmost importance. However, during the early years of modern political theory state appeared to be a machine and the machine was considered to be powerful. To sum up, in the modern traditional period the state has primarily been viewed as a machine and the inner meaning is that the state has been set up to fulfill certain limited functions just like machine. A particular machine is manufactured to do a particular job.

Individualism and Democracy:

Individualism and democracy received tremendous encouragement and support from the writings of a number of thinkers many of whom were well known. In the political thought of Hobbes and Locke individualism was greatly emphasized. Both the contract thinkers considered various rights as of prime importance. Though Hobbes was a great monarchist and not a democrat in our sense, he treated people's right to take food and medicine very important.

Hobbes also said that no authority had any power to force man form taking food and medicine. Priority was always given to man and his all round development and it was firmly believed that if the importance of state is not brought to minimum level individual's freedom could never be achieved and mainly for that reason in Western democracy man was always given utmost importance.

In this period theory of natural rights was treated with special care. It was believed that since the state was not the creator of rights it cannot take them away from individuals.

It was also strongly argued that individual and his rights existed before the establishment of civil society and government and because of this the rights of man must always get first importance. In this way in the stage of modern political theory individual was deliberately brought into the limelight. The best way to protect the rights of individuals is to bind both with contract.

The political thinkers of modern traditional period also focused their attention on individualism because they thought that non-interference on the activities of man was the best for man's progress. It was thought that only democracy was a viable form of government and through it people can develop their inherent qualities.

It is said that though Hobbes was a worshipper of absolutism it cannot be assertively said that he hated democracy. Locke, Rousseau and a score of thinkers were staunch believers of democracy though the forms they advocated were not uniform types. In this connection we can remember Jefferson's famous dictum that government governs best that governs least. Today what we call minimal state in the early modern period that concept was advocated by many celebrities and Jefferson was one of them.

Emancipation of individual became practically the core idea of many political philosophers. Wasby writes "Modern democracy the rise of Protestantism and the development of capitalism are all associated with the emancipation of the individual in Western political thought". Hence democracy and individualism in this period developed simultaneously. But these two concepts were not the solitary occupiers of the entire thought system of this period. Democracy was viewed from different standpoints.

Capitalism and Marxism:

Two important tributaries of political theory that earned prominence in the modern period are capitalism and Marxism. Several states of Western Europe witnessed unprecedented changes in social, political and economic fields in the second half of the eighteenth century and those changes were considered the tangible products of Industrial Revolution.

Industrial Revolution generated fabulous amount of wealth and goods but a major part of which went to a microscopic fraction of society who used it for its own consumption and for further generation of wealth. Through this from the very beginning of nineteenth century developed a new phenomenon which is popularly known as capitalism. The most unpopular product of capitalism is the inequality of income and wealth.

This inequality of wealth and income created a lot of resentment among a large number of thinkers and Karl Marx tops the list. He squarely blamed capitalism for the growing misery of working class. He also believed that the bourgeois state machinery was manipulated by the capitalists in their favour.

Marx's sweeping conclusion was that only a protracted class struggle and permanent revolution can emancipate the common people from the exploitation of capitalist class. From Marxism there arose another doctrine which constituted a very important aspect of modern political theory and it is socialism. Some of its forms are Scientific Socialism, Fabian Socialism etc.

Idealism:

While exploring the various facets of political theory, it would never be prudent to ignore idealism which once upon a time was popular and at the same time formed an important part of political theory. Idealism was first explained and vigorously argued by Plato and Aristotle and later on it received elaborate treatment at the hands of German philosophers, Kant (1724-1804), Hegel (1770-1831) and Fichte (1762- 1814) and Oxford idealists. Idealism is opposed to empiricism. The doctrine propounds that knowledge and sense cannot be derived from experience but from thought.

Idealism also believes that certain eternal values and principles are of vital importance and they have developed through ages and their evolution has reached a stage which cannot be questioned and challenged. These values and principles are manifested in the state to which the individuals must display absolute obedience.

It also preaches that individuals are basically rational and they want fuller blossoming of the values, ideals, ethical and moral principles and according to idealism, this ambitious objective can be achieved through the membership of state. Up to the first half of the nineteenth century, Idealists' philosophy occupied a niche in the whole gamut of political theory. Idealism has various interpretations and versions, but the mere fact is that its association with political theory is a fait accompli.

Nationalism:

The involvement of nationalism with political theory may be contested by many, but a scrutiny of the various aspects of political theory reveals that its association with political theory cannot be ruled out. The nationalist feeling, the concept of nation, state, urge for right to self-determination etc. were all very much active behind the emergence of nationalism.

If we look at the history of Western political thought we shall find that in the fields of nationalism and nation state Machiavelli was the pioneer. In The Prince he advised the prince to unify the various parts of Italy by any means and to establish a nation-state. In fact, nationalism or nation-state per se help flourish the political theory, but its multi faceted developments helped political theory to thrive and one such facet is the concept of sovereignty.

The indomitable urge of the industrialised nations of Europe to dominate the vast territories of Africa and Asia inflamed the nationalist feeling of the people of Asia and Africa. Almond and Powell have rightly observed that in the first-half of the twentieth century, there was a clear absence of political theory and political developments that took place in the Third world states.

These developments were the outcomes of nationalism. This leads to the birth of comparative politics. However, the fact is that the rise and development of nationalism have assisted the progress of political theory. Today comparative politics is an integral part of political theory and their integration has enriched political science to a considerable extent.

Modern Period: Empiricism:

Factors Contributing to the Emergence of Empiricism:

After the Second World War (1939-1945) some top ranking political thinkers of America took a venture to explain the subject by borrowing techniques from different science subjects. This attempt laid the foundation of a new approach to the study of political science.

In the second place, the rapid advance of Marxism in the first few decades of the twentieth century and particularly after the Bolshevik Revolution (1917) in Russia created panic in the minds of political scientists and educationists. The main cause of the panic was that the rapid advance of Marxism and socialist thought was about to expose the real picture of capitalism which was exploitative in nature. To the protagonists of capitalism this was a potent cause of anxiety and tension.

They apprehended that socialism might dethrone capitalism from its present position. All of them decided to combat this situation in an academic way. They thought that a confidence should be created in the minds of people that liberal political thought was much superior to Marxism and in order to do that liberal political analysis must be based on scientific methods and this mentality created a tremendous impact upon the way of explaining the subject.

Thirdly, in the 1940s, a good number of scholars and political scientists from Europe migrated to America and their intention was to introduce new methods of analysis. This point has been aptly pointed out by a critic in the following way, "Beginning in the 1940s, the basic values of American political science were fundamentally challenged by an ideologically diverse group of emigre scholars who coalesced around the project of initiating the first root and branch critique of the discipline".

All of them defended that the discipline must be explained scientifically. This strong determination brought sea changes in the methods of analysis and the fact is that the attempt brought good results.

Fourthly, the Cold War and other connected factors stressed upon science. It was believed in those days that only a proper cultivation of science could yield good and desirable results. Scholars and educationists of USA began to perceive science not simply as an end but also a means and the means would be used to achieve perfection or improvement. Scientists invested their energy and genius to make war weapons more destructive. Political scientists wanted to improve the method of analysis.

Another reason is the traditional political theory for long periods of time revolved around norms and values which means that political science is a normative science. Its emphasis on "is" and "ought" was so important and the penchant for that emphasis made political theory unattractive. Many scholars decided to improve the methods of analysis. Just at that time the Rockefeller Foundation launched a project to facilitate the research of mass communication and American Political Science Association came forward to take this lucrative opportunity.

The purpose was to lay the foundation of a "value-free operational language of political enquiry and as an exercise in scientific political theory". The Rockefeller foundation wanted thorough and fruitful research on the conflict between liberal political theory and the Bolshevik or Marxist approach to political theory.

It also wanted to make a thorough inquiry on war, famine, atomic destruction and their collective impact upon the study of political theory. Two important alternatives appeared before the researchers—to scrupulously adhere to the traditional value added political theory or to posit the theory on scientific foundation and the second alternative finally triumphed. From the 1950s we witness the triumphant advance of empirical analysis of political theory.

Postmodernism:

Another offshoot of modern political theory is post-modernism. It is difficult to define this concept precisely. Since the 1950s political theory was embraced by a new phenomenon which is called postmodernism. It implies that there is nothing like certainty, absolute and universal truth. The whole world is changing as well as outlook and behaviour of individuals and in such situation nothing can be fixed or permanent. It emphasizes on discourse, debate and democracy.

The important feature of postmodernism is that "it stands for the end of science, the death of history, the elimination of objectivity and the very idea of truth, the denial of the world of things and events, the end of cause and effect". Another critic has put the concept in the following words, "As a tool of social and political analysis postmodernism highlights the shift away from societies structured by industrialisation and class solidarity to increasingly fragmented and pluralistic information societies".

We thus see that postmodernism believes in atomic individualism. In its opinion individual is the only final determiner of everything. It denies the authority. But post modernism is silent about anarchism. However, its view leads to anarchist structure of society.

Rational Choice Theory:

Origin and Central Idea:

In the fifties and sixties of the last century political theory witnessed a new development in its own arena and it is popularly known as rational choice theory. In modern time the theory found its roots in the analysis of Hobbes who said that society with a government of absolute powers far better than state of nature. Here is a clear choice of individuals. Because of certain deficiencies people preferred civil society to state of nature.

There are clear hints of the theory in the writings of other thinkers. The rational choice theory originated in Anthony Dawn's noted book An Economic Theory of Democracy (1957). Duncan Black published The Theory of Committee and Elections in 1958. Herbert Simon's Models of Man was published in 1957. Between 1957 and 1973 there were published a number of books which deal with rational choice.

The central idea of the doctrine is when a man or group of men are given a number of alternatives they, after calculating all the aspects, decide a particular course of action. That is, they arrive at a decision. Behind the arrival of the decision rationality of the person concerned plays a vital role. In other words, rationality is the chief guiding force and because of this it is called rational choice theory.

By the mid-1970s the theory was very popular and it was first applied to economics and then political scientists took interest. Hence the central idea of the rational choice theory of politics is reason or rationality is the main determiner of people's choice. Moved by rationality men select an action.

Features of the Theory:

From what has been said by its proponents certain features can be derived. One such feature is there is an identifiable set of actions which lead to an identifiable set of outcomes or results of these actions. Here the word identifiable is very important. Both actions and outcomes can be identified. In the second place the participants in the actions are rational and reasonable and they can order the preferences considering outcome. They can identify the actions and at the same time the consequences.

This enables them to take a particular course of action. In the third place, several alternatives are placed before the participants or actors and they are given the freedom to choose any one of the alternatives. In the fourth place, the actors or participants select that alternative which can assure the maximum benefit or utility.

In the fifth place, while selecting the alternative the actor applies his intelligence or reason so that he can arrive at a comfortable or viable position. In the sixth place, the rational choice model assures that while going to select a particular alternative the individual is not faced with any restriction the meaning of which is he enjoys full freedom.

Finally, the rational choice model starts with the individual level and reaches the collective level. That is, from micro level to macro level. The rational choice level is the hyphen between micro and macro levels.

Assessment:

The rational choice theory has been subjected to a number of criticisms. It gives emphasis on alternatives and their outcomes. The problem is what is the exact number of the alternatives and their outcomes? The advocates of the theory cannot throw light on this issue and this creates confusion and deficiency.

The supporters of the theory claim that it can help the researchers to arrive at a fruitful discussion of politics and political theory will get inspiration from it. But critics are of opinion that since the back bone of the theory is rationality this very rationality can be questioned. How many individuals possess the rationality?

Heywood observes: "In proceeding from an abstract model of individual, rational choice theory pays insufficient attention to social and historical factors". There is another objection. For the proper functioning of the theory a liberal or democratic set up of the society is essential.

All the individuals or at least the rational persons will be given sufficient freedom to select the most desirable alternatives so that he/she can maximise his/her utility or benefit. But such an atmosphere is not easily available. It is alleged that the doctrine may effectively work at the micro level, but its success at the macro level is not encouraging at all.

A clash of interest, choices and tastes is inevitable and how is an equilibrium to be attained? Its advocates cannot assure us on this issue. There is still a limitation of the theory. For the development of rationality or reason education and favourable circumstances are required which are not easily available.

The Task of Political Theory:

We have very briefly surveyed the revival or resurgence of political theory in the 1950s and 1960s. A pertinent question which peeps into our mind is why a large number of political scientists and researchers took so much trouble and time to do the research work for the resurgence of political theory? The answer to this vexed question lies in the importance or task of political theory.

Almond, Powell, David Easton, Robert Dahl, Lasswell and Kaplan etc. took special care in regard to the comprehensive analysis of political system which the traditional thinkers avoided. Easton says: "For a variety of reasons a theoretical frame work is essential to an adequate analysis of political system". Only a systematic and well-built theory is capable of identifying the important political variables and analysing the relations among them.

In the second place, according to Easton a political theory "maps out the areas in which additional or new research is badly needed". Finally, a political theory "adds to the reliability of the results of both new and old research in a way impossible without the existence of a relatively consistent body of concepts".

The function of a political theory (some critics call general theory though there is difference between the two), is to construct a conceptual framework through which to make sense of disparate phenomena.

Classification of Political Theory:

Value Theory and Causal Theory:

The political scientists of the second half of the twentieth century were quite conscious of the importance of theory and remembering this they framed a structure of political theory. Easton says that a theory is used to mean many things. In the first place according to Easton a theory is used for explaining the values or philosophical aspects of politics.

Here the word value is used not in the sense of economics, but in philosophical or moral or ethical sense. In cases more than one theory is used to indicate value. Easton calls it Value Theory. We can say value comprises a part of political theory and in that sense it is called Value Theory.

There is a second type of theory designated by Easton and it called Causal Theory. A causal theory is one which is used to find out a relation between facts. The researcher collects facts and tries to find out relationship among them and while doing so in his mind there is always a picture of theory which is quite active.

Easton points out the importance of causal theory in the following words: "The importance of causal theory lies in the fact that it is an index of the stage of development of any science, social or physical, towards the attainment of reliable knowledge. Very briefly, causal theory is a device for improving the dependability of our knowledge".

Factual Theory:

For building up of a theory, it is essential that facts are to be collected and analysed. But mere collection of facts is not enough, their analysis is also important and for that purpose theoretical knowledge is also essential. Before entering into a detailed analysis we want to define facts and we shall do it in the words of Easton: "A fact is a particular ordering of reality in terms of a theoretical interest".

But the collection of facts or data like a blind man is not enough. While collecting data or facts sufficient intelligence and knowledge are to be applied because only with the help of facts and data we can build up the foundation of a theory. When a researcher collects facts and data, he carries with him a clear picture and frame of a theory and on the basis of that, he starts his work of collecting facts. For this reason, Easton says—"Facts therefore imply duty".

In Easton's analysis of factual theory, we further observe that facts and data are to be collected with a good deal of acumen and after that two functions are to be performed. One is the relationship among the data is to be established and the other is facts and data are to be generalised. "Every generalisation," Easton continues, "is in a sense a theory, it is a statement of relationship which is only probably, not certainly and finally, true". Facts and data are to be critically examined.

Three Propositions:

Easton discusses the political theory in the light of behaviouralism. He is of opinion that though there are differences in the political behaviour of individuals, a close observation reveals that there are also uniformities in the political behaviour and on the basis of those uniformities the political scientists form generalisations and theory. Easton points out three such forms. One is Singular Generalisation. Second is Narrow Gauge theory and the third is Broad Gauge theory.

In Easton's opinion, the Singular Generalisations are not in the strict sense theories. The researcher collects uniform behaviour of individuals and after analysing them prepares at certain conclusions or we can say he forms generalisations. Easton calls it singular generalisations.

The political scientist analyses very few variables and on the basis of that he forms generalisations. This approach is not a sufficient way of framing an acceptable theory.

Singular generalisations are the primary level of a political theory and it is not surprising that he does not call it a political theory.

At the higher level there is a Narrow Gauge Theory. It is also called Synthetic Theory. In the words of Easton the narrow gauge theory "consists of a set of interrelated propositions that are designed to synthesise the data contained in an unorganised body of singular generalisations".

The supporters of the narrow gauge theory are accustomed to viewing political theory and political science in terms of power enunciated by Lasswell. He viewed political science as simply the study of the struggle of or for power. According to Lasswell, in any society there are various groups and consequently many centres of power. Each group or each centre always tries to capture power by defeating the other group.

This is particularly the characteristic feature of any pluralist society. According to Lasswell and several others, power always remains at the centre of any political analysis because no society can be analysed without power. The narrow gauge theory, no doubt, is broader than the singular generalisation, but it is not really broad because power can never be the central theme of a theory.

Finally, there is a Broad Gauge Theory. It can also be called Systematic Theory. Hierarchically viewed broad gauge theory is at the highest stage of the whole series. It is neither narrow nor singular. In the considered judgment of Easton in any society there occur large number of incidents and facts and all these are not relevant for any political scientist. Only few or selective facts or data may be useful for him.

Here the problem is how he will select these facts and data? Before a political scientist starts to collect and analyse data and facts he forms a conceptual framework and this acts as a guidance. The conceptual framework is a kind of sieve which selects data and facts.

Status of Political Theory:

We have already noted that the gravest charge against the traditional political theory is—it is extremely reluctant to apply improved and sophisticated methods of other - sciences, particularly natural sciences. If the traditional political theory could do that it would have been able to improve its status as a branch of science subjects such as economics and psychology.

Many serious persons and policy-makers refuse to put political science or political theory, economics, psychology and several other subjects within the same bracket. It is lamented that since political scientists do not use sophisticated data, its conclusions have failed to satisfy many.

Easton says that political theory as well as political science has not been able to establish itself as a distinct branch of social science. In earlier epochs, large number of persons associated with the disciplines treated it as a branch of history or economics and this was never a matter of prestige for political scientists.

It has been observed that this lower status of political theory or political science was chiefly due to the reason that it was not able to draw the attention of serious scholars and researchers. But Easton claims that "Political Science does constitute a distinct field of research, not for problems of application alone, but, what is more significant, for analytical and conceptual purposes as well".

For the enhancement of status, utility, importance, etc. of a discipline it is essential that it (the discipline) must construct a theoretical framework and political theory up to the fifties has not been able to do that. Easton concludes that political science must accept that venture boldly.

Again, prediction is an important function of a science subject. Subjects of social science in general and political science in particular are not always able to make proper predictions. But that drawback must not be over-emphasized. Political Theory can be elevated to that status and for that purpose, political theory must be made a comprehensive theory.

Let us again quote Easton. "Where research has been quantitatively and qualitatively adequate to permit of prediction its success is geared neatly to the existence of a comprehensive body of consistent theory". If a comprehensive and consistent theory exists prediction becomes feasible.

Easton's main point is that to enable political theory to make prediction its research work must be improved and must be made a distinct discipline. During the first half of the twentieth century, there was a lot of resentment in the academic world of political science in America because of the inadequacy of research in this subject. A large number of political scientists have however been able to change it.

In conclusion few words may be added. If we go through the various concepts, approaches and models prepared by the political scientists we shall witness an interesting fact. Time has not yet arrived to say anything about the subject (political science) assertively. The excessive stress on values, judgment and norms was challenged by empiricists. Again in the seventies there has occurred a revival of traditionalism and it is highly prominent in Rawls' analysis of justice.

In his revised version of behaviouralism (which is popularly knows post-behaviouralism), Easton argued in favour of values and norms. Postmodernism puts a challenge to both traditionalism and empiricism. It claims that there is not such thing as absolute or universal truth, norms and values. It even challenges the social and economic structure of society based on industrialisation.

From 1950s to 1990s, people renewed their faith on socialism but the collapse of the erstwhile Soviet Union has destroyed that faith.

CHAPTER TWO

DEMOCRACY

What is Democracy?

Democracy means rule by the people. The name is employed for various sorts of government, where the people can participate within the decisions that affect the way their community is run. A democratic government is a system of government that is elected by the whole adult population, people over the age of 18 years. They do this by choosing someone to represent their community at an area, state and federal level. The purpose of the elected government is to protect the people and promote their rights, interests, and welfare to the benefit of everyone.

Where the term democracy derives from?

The word democracy originated in ancient Greece over 2400 years ago.

'**Demos**' means common people and '**Kratos**' means strength.

Democracy as we know it today as freedom system of government in which citizens exercise power directly or elect representatives from amongst themselves. The term democracy first appeared in ancient Greek political and philosophical Fort in the city state of Athens during classical antiquity even the word democracy comes from the agent Greek language demos meaning people and kratos meaning strength, Athenians established what is generally held is the first democracy in 580 - 507 BC.

Cleisthenes is known as the father of Athenian democracy. Athenian democracy took the form of a direct democracy and it had to distinguishing features the random selection of ordinary citizens to fill the few existing government, administrative and judicial officers and the legislative assembly consisting of all the senior citizens. All eligible citizens were allowed to speak and vote in the assembly, which set the laws of the city state. However opinion citizenship excluded women slaves and foreigners, so wasn't that free of world in voters we know today, but it was a good start.

The Roman Republic contributed significantly to many aspects of democracy only a minority of Romans for citizens with votes in elections for representatives additionally the Roman model of governments inspired many political thinkers, health centuries and days modern representative democracies imitate more the Roman, the Greek models because it was a state in which supreme power was held by the people and their elected representatives and which had an elected or nominated leader. Another example that the natives in North America which between around 1450 -1680 AD also develop the form of democratic society before they came in contact with the Europeans. This indicates the forms of democracy may have been invented in other societies around the world. In medieval times, most regions in Europe or ruled by clergy or future loads, almost no democracy remain from the ancient Greeks or Romans in the parliament.

The first English parliament was created in 1265 starting separation of powers in state many laws and rules are made after this event in the whole of Europe. The power of kings began to fade to local nobles and afterwards to the people after some centuries the case of proclamations in 1610 in England decided that the king by his proclamation or other ways cannot change any part of the common law or statute law all the customs of the realm awesome after World War One. Austria-Hungary and the Ottoman Empire collapse giving the opportunity to oppressed nations to be free in 1918, the United Kingdom granted the right to vote to women and in 1928 granted women and men equal rights. In 1920 women stop the right to vote in the United States and in 1944 in France. In 1920, the US for granted full US citizenship to Americas indigenous peoples.

History of direct Democracy

One strand of thought sees direct democracy as common and widespread in pre-state societies.

The earliest well-documented direct democracy is claimed to be the Athenian democracy of the 5th century BC. The main bodies within the Athenian democracy were the assembly, composed of male citizens; the boul, composed of 500 citizens; and therefore the law courts, composed of a huge number of jurors chosen by lot, with no judges. Ancient Attica had only about 30,000 male citizens, but several thousand of them were politically active in each year and many of them quite regularly for years on end. The Athenian democracy was direct not only within the sense that the assembled people made decisions, but also within the sense that the people - through the assembly, boul, and law courts - controlled the whole political process, and an outsized proportion of citizens were involved constantly in publicly affairs. Most modern democracies, being representative, not direct, don't resemble the Athenian system.

Also relevant to the history of direct democracy is that the history of Ancient Rome, specifically during the Roman Republic, traditionally founded around 509 BC. Rome displayed many aspects of democracy, both direct and indirect, from the age of Roman monarchy all the thanks to the collapse of the Roman Empire.

While the Roman senate was the most body with historical longevity, lasting from the Roman kingdom until after the collapse of the Western Roman Empire in 476 AD, it did not embody a purely democratic approach, being made up - during the late republic - of former elected officials, providing advice instead of creating law.

The democratic aspect of the constitution resided within the Roman popular assemblies, where the people organised into centuriae or into tribes - counting on the assembly - and cast votes on various matters, including elections and laws, proposed before them by their elected magistrates. Some classicists have argued that the Roman Republic deserves the label of **democracy**, with universal suffrage for man citizens, popular sovereignty and transparent deliberation of public affairs. Many historians mark the top of the Republic with the lex Titia, passed on 27 November 43 BC, which eliminated many oversight provisions.

Ultramodern Direct Republic also occurs within the Crow Nation, a Native American Tribe in the United States of America. The lineage is organized around a General Council formed of all voting- age members. The General Council has the power to produce fairly - binding opinions through blackballs. The General Council was first elevated in the 1948 Crow Constitution and was upheld and re-instated with the 2002 Constitution.

Some of the issues girding the affiliated notion of a direct republic using the Internet and other dispatches technologies are dealt with in the composition one-democracy and below under the heading Electronic direct republic. Further compactly, the conception of open-source governance applies principles of the free software movement to the governance of people, allowing the entire crowd to share in government directly, as much or as little as they please.

Direct republic is the base of challenger and left-libertarian political study. Direct republic has been supported by challenger thinkers since its commencement, and direct republic as a political proposition has been largely told by anarchism.

A democracy is a form of government that empowers the people to exercise political control, limits the power of the head of state, provides for the <u>separation of powers</u> between governmental entities, and ensures the protection of <u>natural rights</u> and <u>civil liberties</u>. In practice, democracy takes many different forms. Along with the two most common types of democracies—direct and representative—variants such as participatory, liberal, parliamentary, pluralist, constitutional, and socialist democracies can be found in use today.

Key Takeaways: Democracy

- Democracy, literally meaning "rule by the people," empowers individuals to exercise political control over the form and functions of their government.
- While democracies come in several forms, they all feature competitive elections, <u>freedom of expression</u>, and protection of individual civil liberties and human rights.
- In most democracies, the needs and wishes of the people are represented by elected lawmakers who are charged with writing and voting on laws and setting policy.
- When creating laws and policies, the elected representatives in a democracy strive to balance conflicting demands and obligations to maximize freedom and protect individual rights.

Despite the prominence in the headlines of non-democratic, authoritarian states like China, Russia, North Korea, and Iran, democracy remains the world's most commonly practiced form of government. In 2018, for example, a total of 96 out of 167 countries (57%) with populations of at least 500,000 were democracies of some type. Statics show that the percentage of democracies among the world's governments has been increasing since the mid-1970s, currently standing just short of its post-World War II high of 58% in 2016.

A democracy is a form of government that empowers the people to exercise political control, limits the power of the head of state, provides for the separation of powers between governmental entities, and ensures the protection of natural rights and civil liberties. In practice, democracy takes many different forms. Along with the two most common types of democracies—direct and representative—variants such as participatory, liberal, parliamentary, pluralist, constitutional, and socialist democracies can be found in use today.

Democratic Principles

While their opinions vary, a consensus of political scientists agree that most democracies are based on six foundational elements:

- Popular sovereignty: The principle that the government is created and maintained by the consent of the people through their elected representatives.

- An Electoral System: Since according to the principle of popular sovereignty, the people are the source of all political power, a clearly defined system of conducting free and fair elections is essential.
- Public Participation: Democracies rarely survive without the active participation of the people. Health democracies enable and encourage the people to take part in their political and civic processes.
- Separation of Powers: Based on a suspicion of power concentrated in a single individual—like a king—or group, the constitutions of most democracies provide that political powers be separated and shared among the various governmental entities.
- Human Rights: Along with their constitutionally enumerated rights freedoms, democracies protect the human rights of all citizens. In this context, human rights are those rights considered inherent to all human beings, regardless of nationality, sex, national or ethnic origin, color, religion, language, or any other considerations.
- A Rule of Law: Also called due process of law, the rule of law is the principle that all citizens are accountable to laws that are publicly created and equitably enforced in a manner consistent with human rights by an independent judicial system.

Democracy Definition

According to Abraham Lincoln, "Democracy is **a government of the people, by the people, and for the**

people."

Meaning "rule by the people," democracy is a system of government that not only allows but requires the participation of the people in the political process to function properly. U.S. President Abraham Lincoln, in his famed 1863 Gettysburg Address may have best-defined democracy as a "...government of the people, by the people, for the people..."

Semantically, the term democracy comes from the Greek words for "people" (dēmos) and "rule" (karatos). However, achieving and preserving a government by the people—a "popular" government—is far more complicated than the concept's semantic simplicity might imply. In creating the legal framework under which the democracy will function, typically a constitution, several crucial political and practical questions must be answered.

Is "rule by the people" even appropriate for the given state? Do the inherent freedoms of a democracy justify dealing with its complex bureaucracy and electoral processes, or would the streamlined predictability of a monarchy, for example, be preferable?

Assuming a preference for democracy, which residents of the country, state, or town should enjoy the political status of full citizenship? Simply stated, who are the "people" in the "government by the people" equation? In the United States, for example, the constitutionally established doctrine of birthright citizenship provides that any person born on U.S. soil automatically becomes a U.S. citizen. Other democracies are more restrictive in bestowing full citizenship.

Which people within the democracy should be empowered to participate in it? Assuming that only adults are allowed to fully participate in the political process, should all adults be included? For example, until the enactment of the 19th Amendment in 1920, women in the United States were not allowed to vote in national elections. A democracy that excludes too many of the governed from taking part in what is supposed to be their government runs the risk of becoming an aristocracy—government by a small, privileged ruling class—or an oligarchy—government by an elite, typically wealthy, few.

If, as one of the foundational principles of democracy holds, the majority rules, what will a "proper" majority be? A majority of all citizens or a majority of citizens who vote only? When issues, as they inevitably will, divide the people, should the wishes of the majority always prevail, or should, as in the case of the American Civil Rights Movement, minorities be empowered to overcome majority rule? Most importantly, what legal or legislative mechanisms should be created to prevent the democracy from becoming a victim of what one of America's Founding Fathers, James Madison, called "the tyranny of the majority?"

Finally, how likely is it that a majority of the people will continue to believe that democracy is the best form of government for them? For a democracy to survive it must retain the substantial support of both the people and the leaders they choose. History has shown that democracy is a particularly fragile institution. In fact, of the 120 new democracies that have emerged around the world since 1960, nearly half have resulted in failed states or have been replaced by other, typically more authoritarian forms of government. It is therefore essential that democracies be designed to respond quickly and appropriately to the internal and external factors that will inevitably threaten them.

According to Dicey, "Democracy is **a form of government in which the governing body is a comparatively large fraction of the entire nation**".

According to Seeley: - "Democracy is **a government in which every one has a share**."

In the Dictionary Definition, "Democracy is a government by the people in which the supreme power is vested in the people and exercised directly by them or by their elected agents under a free electoral system."

Types of Democracy

Throughout history, more types of democracy have been identified than there are countries in the world. According to social and political philosopher Jean-Paul Gagnon, more than 2,234 adjectives have been used to describe democracy. While many scholars refer to direct and representative as the most common of these, several other types of democracies can be found around the world today. While direct democracy is unique, most other recognized types of democracy are variants of representative democracy.

These various types of democracy are generally descriptive of the particular values emphasized by the representative democracies that employ them.

Direct Democracy

Originated in <u>Ancient Greece</u> during the 5th century BCE, <u>direct democracy</u>, sometimes called "pure democracy," is considered the oldest non-authoritarian form of government. In a direct democracy, all laws and public policy decisions are made directly by a majority vote of the people, rather than by the votes of their elected representatives.

Functionally possible only in small states, Switzerland is the only example of a direct democracy applied on a national level today. While Switzerland is no longer a true direct democracy, any law passed by the popularly elected national parliament can be vetoed by a direct vote of the public. Citizens can also change the constitution through direct votes on amendments. In the United States, examples of direct democracy can be found in state-level recall elections and law-making <u>ballot initiatives</u>.

Representative

Also called indirect democracy, <u>representative democracy</u> is a system of government in which all eligible citizens elect officials to pass laws and formulate public policy on their behalf. These elected officials are expected to represent the needs and viewpoints of the people in deciding the best course of action for the nation, state, or other jurisdiction as a whole.

As the most commonly found type of democracy in use today, almost 60% of all countries employ some form of representative democracy including the United States, the United Kingdom, and France.

Participatory

In a participatory democracy, the people vote directly on policy while their elected representatives are responsible for implementing those policies. Participatory democracies rely on the citizens in setting the direction of the state and the operation of its political systems. While the two forms of government share similar ideals, participatory democracies tend to encourage a higher, more direct form of citizen participation than traditional representative democracies.

While there are no countries specifically classified as participatory democracies, most representative democracies employ citizen participation as a tool for social and political reform. In the United States, for example, so-called "grassroots" citizen participation causes such as the Civil Rights Movement of the 1960s have led elected officials to enact laws implementing sweeping social, legal, and political policy changes.

Liberal

Liberal democracy is loosely defined as a form of representative democracy that emphasizes the principles of classical liberalism—an ideology advocating the protection of individual civil liberties and economic freedom by limiting the power of the government. Liberal democracies employ a constitution, either statutorily codified, as in the United States or uncodified, as in the United Kingdom, to define the powers of the government, provide for a separation of those powers, and enshrine the social contract.

Liberal democracies may take the form of a constitutional republic, like the United States, or a constitutional monarchy, such as the United Kingdom, Canada, and Australia.

Parliamentary

In a parliamentary democracy, the people directly elect representatives to a legislative parliament. Similar to the U.S. Congress, the parliament directly represents the people in making necessary laws and policy decisions for the country.

In parliamentary democracies such as the United Kingdom, Canada, and Japan, the head of government is a prime minister, who is first elected to parliament by the people, then elected prime minister by a vote of the parliament. However, the prime minister remains a member of the parliament and thus plays an active role in the legislative process of creating and passing laws. Parliamentary democracies are typically a feature of a constitutional monarch, a system of government in which the head of state is a queen or king, whose power is limited by a constitution.

Pluralist

In a pluralist democracy, no single group dominates politics. Instead, organized groups within the people compete to influence public policy. In political science, the term pluralism expresses the ideology that influence should be spread among different interest groups, rather than held by a single elite group as in an aristocracy. Compared to participatory democracies, in which individuals take part in influencing political decisions, in a pluralist democracy, individuals work through groups formed around common causes hoping to win the support of elected leaders.

In this context, the pluralist democracy assumes that the government and the society as a whole benefit from a diversity of viewpoints. Examples of pluralist democracy can be seen in the impact, special interest groups, such as the National Organization for Women, have had on American politics.

Constitutional

While the exact definition continues to be debated by political scientists, constitutional democracy is generally defined as a system of government based on popular sovereignty and a rule of law in which the structures, powers, and limits of government are established by a constitution. Constitutions are intended to restrict the power of the government, typically by separating those powers between the various branches of government, as in the United States' constitution's system of federalism. In a constitutional democracy, the constitution is considered to be the "supreme law of the land."

Socialist

Democratic socialism is broadly defined as a system of government based on a socialist economy, in which most property and means of production are collectively, rather than individually, controlled by a constitutionally established political hierarchy—the government. Social democracy embraces government regulation of business and industry as a means of furthering economic growth while preventing income inequality.

While there are no purely socialist governments in the world today, elements of democratic socialism can be seen in Sweden's provision of free universal health care, education, and sweeping social welfare programs.

Necessary Conditions for the Successful Working of Democracy

The following conditions are necessary for the successful working of Democracy-

- **Belief in Democratic Principles-** The first condition necessary for the successful working of democracy is that citizens of that country should have faith in democratic principles. They should have respect for other views and should perform their duties properly.
- **Economic Equality-** Democracy can function smoothly in countries that do not have extremes of wealth and property. A country in which a large number of persons

are poor while a few of them have plenty cannot run democratic institutions successfully.

- **Educated Citizens-** Only educated citizens can have knowledge of their rights and duties and can exercise them properly. Uneducated citizens cannot even cast their votes properly.
- **High Moral Standard-** Democracy can be run successfully in a country whose citizens are honest, impartial and selfless. They should not be amenable to undue pressures during elections.
- **Right Types of Leaders-** The success of democracy depends greatly on the quality of leaders a country is able to provide. Leaders must be men of sound judgement, balanced mind, honest and of unimpeachable character.
- **Equal Social and Political Rights-** Democracy can be successful if all the citizens are given equal social and political rights. Equality before the law, the right to vote and to fight elections should be given to all.
- **Sound Party System-** Democracy can be successful in a country where political parties are organized on definite economic, social and political principles and not on the basis of religion or caste.
- **Free and Honest Press-** A free press is said to be the Bible of democracy. The people should have access to free and unbiased information regarding domestic and foreign affairs.
- **Independent Judiciary-** Independent Judiciary is also necessary for the successful working of democracy. If the judiciary is not free and independent, the right and liberties of the citizens cannot be safeguarded.
- **Local-Self Government-** In order to make democracy successful, local institutions should be established at all

levels. Local institutions (Municipalities, Panchayats etc.) serve as the training ground for democracy.

- **Strong Opposition-** Strong and organized opposition is also necessary for the successful working of democracy. It checks the government from becoming dictatorial.
- **Peace and Security-** Democracy can run successfully in a country where peace and security prevail. In countries that have the perpetual danger of war or revolt, democracy cannot be run successfully.

Differences between Democracy and Dictatorship

Democracy

- A democracy is a form of government in which the people possess the ultimate power.
- Democracy believes in Equality.
- It encourages free thoughts.
- People choose what is good for them.
- People can change, create and enact the laws.

Dictatorship

- Dictatorship is a form of government in which rulers possesses all the powers.
- Dictatorship believes in hierarchy.
- It suppresses free thoughts and actions.
- A dictator imposes what he/she thinks is good for his/her rule.
- Laws is created by the dictator with no involvement of the people.

CHAPTER THREE

LIBERTY

The concept of Freedom or Liberty is complex with strong emotional connotations. The terms has acquired different meaning at different times. Still there is a common thread through all its usages.

The most important sense in which liberty is used is when a rational person is able to exercise his choice without being subject to any external constraint. In this sense, liberty is a necessary condition for free and full development of our personality. Without it, we cannot be rational or act or achieve what seems best to us. To have liberty is to be able to act according to one's wishes. To translate it is one's dreams into reality and to realize one's potential. It is the essence of humanity and provides substance to the notion of responsibility. It is the ideal to which all of us aspire.

A man is free if he is not prohibited by others. Liberty may also mean freedom to do something or enjoying one's powers. When we are able to do what to do, we are said to be free. It may mean immunity from authority's exercise of authority powers. It means freedom to act independently without any fear of punishment. Then there is freedom under law. Citizens have liberty in so far as what law permits them to do or not to do.

Why do we need constraints

Man is by nature a social being. He wants to live with others. So the first condition of common living and co-operative life is common regulation. Without common rules, co-operative life will be an impossibility. Common rules promote right living and the concept of right living is individual's own conception. So individual will have the scope to decide what is convenient and right. The rules therefore safeguard liberty from the interference of other persons or authority.

The purpose of constraints is not to curtail or abolish freedom but to preserve and enlarge it. Where there is no constraint, violence and anarchy will prevail jeopardizing the cultivation of liberty. So constraints are essential components of freedom.

Absence of constraint may enhance the scope of liberty of one or few or whatever it may be. But the total quantum of liberty of all individuals, as a result of absence of constraints, is bound to decrease.

Hence, liberty and constraints can not be separated from each other. The problem of Political Science is how to rationalize and organize the constraints in order to maximize liberty of all individuals. None will be allowed to feel that the constraints are in excess of the liberty he receives from the society. This is a problem of balancing liberty from constraints. Thus dilemma of liberty is, without constraints it carries no validity and again, excessive or undesirable constraints destroys liberty. So it is essential that both the government and the individual will be conscious about liberty and its protection.

Meaning of Liberty

Liberty is derived from a Latin word "Liber" which means free or independent. Being a theme emanating from a normative theory, a precise meaning cannot be arrived by liberty. The concept of liberty occupies a very important place in civics.

It has made powerful appeal to every man in every age. It is the source of many wars and revolutions. In the name of liberty; war, battles, revolutions and struggles have taken place in the history of mankind.

Liberty means the unrestricted freedom of the individual to do anything he likes to do. But this sort of unrestricted liberty is not possible in society.

Liberty is not a license to do anything one pleases, as this would end up in anarchy, the very extreme of liberty. Restrictions are necessary in the interest of general welfare. They are imposed in the form of laws.

Law is the condition of liberty. While laws are restrictions to liberty, it is imperative that, the so imposed laws are not unjust as excessive and stringent restrictions hamper the intellectual and moral growth of the individual.

Liberty has two aspects. They are Negative aspect and Positive aspect.

Definitions of Liberty

"Liberty means the power of doing what we ought to do" - Montesquieu.

"Liberty means the absence of restraints" - Prof Seely.

The meaning of liberty finds its positive affirmation in the thought of T.H. Green who describes it as the power to do or enjoy something that is worth doing or enjoying in common with others. Liberty is the eager maintenance of that atmosphere in which men have the opportunity to be their best selves.

Liberty means the positive power of doing or enjoying - T.H. Green.

Taken together, it must be understood that, liberty exists not merely in the absence of restraints but in the presence of opportunities as well. The following definition embraces both aspects of liberty.

Liberty is the product of Rights. It is the maximum opportunity to do desired things with a minimum of controls and regulations consonant with a well - ordered society.

Kinds of Liberty

To have an easy understanding, Liberty can be stated as a state of freedom especially opposed to political subjection, imprisonment or slavery.

Writers like Mac Iver, Laski and others classified liberty in to specific varieties. They are,

1. Natural Liberty,
2. Social / Civil Liberty,
3. Moral Liberty.

Social / Civil liberty if further classified in to
    1. Person liberty
2. Political Liberty
3. Economic Liberty
4. Domestic Liberty
5. National Liberty
6. International Liberty

1. Natural Liberty :

It implies complete freedom for a man to do what he wills. In other words, it means absence of all restraints and freedom from interferences. It may be easily understood that this kind of liberty is no liberty at all in as much as it is euphemism for the freedom of the forest. What we call liberty pertains to the realm of man's social existence.

This kind of liberty, in the opinions of the social contractualists like Hobbes, Locke and Rousseau was engaged by men living in the state of nature - since where there was no state and society. This kind of liberty is not possible at present. Liberty cannot exist in the absence of state. Unlimited liberty might have
been engaged only by few strong but not all.

2. Social Liberty :

Social liberty relates to man's freedom in his life as a members of the social organization. As such, it refers to a man's right to do what he wills in compliance with the restraints imposed on him in the general interest. Civil or social liberty consists in the rights and privileges that the society recongnizes and the state
protects in the spheres of private and public life of an individual. Social liberty has the following sub categories:

(a) Personal Liberty :

Personal liberty is an important variety of social liberty. It refers to the opportunity to exercises freedom of choice in those areas of a man's life that the results of his efforts mainly affect him in that isolation by which at least he is always surrounded.

(b) Political Liberty :

It refers to the power of the people to be active in the affairs of the state. Political liberty is closely interlinked with the life of man as a citizen.

Simply stated political liberty consists in provisions for universal adult franchise, free and fair elections, freedom for the avenues that make a healthy public opinion. As a matter of fact political liberty consists in curbing as well as constituting and controlling the government.

(c) Economic Liberty :

It belongs to the individual in the capacity of a producer or a worker engaged in some gainful occupation or service. The individual should be free from the constant fear of unemployment and insufficiency.

(d) Domestic Liberty :

It is sociological concept that takes the discussion of liberty to the sphere of man's family life. It implies that all associations within the state, the miniature community of the family is the most universal and of the strongest independent vitality.

Domestic liberty consists in

1. Rendering the wife a fully responsible individual capable of holding property, suing and being sued, conducting business on her own account, and engaging full personal protection against her husband.

2. is establishing marriage as far as the law is concerned on a purely contractual basis, and leaving the sacramental aspect of marriage to the ordinance of the religion professed by the parties and

3. seeing the physical, mental and moral care of the children.

(e) National liberty :

It is synonymous with national independence. As such, it

implies that no nation should be under subjection of another. National movements or wars of independence can be identified as struggles for the attainment of national liberty.

So national liberty is identified with patriotism.

(f) International Liberty :

It means the world is free from controls and limitation, use of force has no value. Dispute can be settled through peaceful means. Briefly all countries in the world will be free of conflicts and wars. Peace will prevail.

In the international sphere, it implies renunciation of war, limitation on the production of armaments, abandonment's of the use of force, and the pacific settlement of disputes. The ideal of international liberty is based on this pious conviction to that extent the world frees itself from the use of force and aggression it gains and peace is given a chance to establish itself.

3. Moral Liberty :

This type of freedom is centered in the idealistic thoughts of thinkers from Plato and Aristotle in ancient times to Rousseau, Kant, Hegel, Green and Bosanquet in modern times. Moral liberty lies in man's capacity to act as per his rational self.

Every man has a personality of his own. He seeks the best possible development of his personality. At the same time he desire the same thing for other. And more than this, he pays sincere respect for the real worth and dignity of his fellow beings. It is directly connected with man's self - realization.

Dimensions of Liberty

Positive and Negative Liberty

Positive liberty is the possession of the power and resources to act in the context of the structural limitations of the broader society which impacts a person's ability to act, as opposed to negative liberty, which is freedom from external restraint on one's actions.

As Heyman notes, it is important to understand Isaiah Berlin's two definitions of liberty in the context of the ideological circumstances of the 1950s, so a conception of positive liberty includes freedom from external constraints, leading to an understanding of positive liberty in the context of human agency.

According to Charles Taylor, Positive liberty is the ability to fulfill one's purposes. Negative liberty is the freedom from interference by others. The concepts of structure and agency are central to the concept of positive liberty because in order to be free, a person should be free from inhibitions of the social structure in carrying out their ambitions.

Structurally, classism, sexism, ageism, ableism and racism can inhibit a person's freedom. As positive liberty is primarily concerned with the possession of sociological agency, it is enhanced by the ability of citizens to participate in government and have their voices, interests, and concerns recognized and acted upon.

Isaiah Berlin's essay "Two Concepts of Liberty" (1958) is typically acknowledged as the

first to explicitly draw the distinction between positive and negative liberty.

Negative liberty is freedom from interference by other people. Negative liberty is primarily concerned with freedom from external restraint and contrasts with positive liberty (the possession of the power and resources to fulfil one's own potential). The distinction was introduced by Isaiah Berlin in his 1958 lecture "Two Concepts of Liberty".

Negative liberty is the absence of obstacles, barriers or constraints. One has negative liberty to the extent that actions are available to one in this negative sense. Positive liberty is the possibility of acting — or the fact of acting — in such a way as to take control of one's life and realize one's fundamental purposes. While negative liberty is usually attributed to individual agents, positive liberty is sometimes attributed to collectivities, or to individuals considered primarily as members of given collectivities.

The idea of distinguishing between a negative and a positive sense of the term 'liberty' goes back at least to Kant, and was examined and defended in depth by Isaiah Berlin in the 1950s and 60s. Discussions about positive and negative liberty normally take place within the context of political and social philosophy. They are distinct from, though sometimes related to, philosophical discussions about free will. Work on the nature of positive liberty often overlaps, however, with work on the nature of autonomy.

As Berlin showed, negative and positive liberty are not merely two distinct kinds of liberty; they can be seen as rival, incompatible interpretations of a single political ideal. Since few people claim to be against liberty, the way this term is interpreted and defined can have important political implications.

Political liberalism tends to presuppose a negative definition of liberty: liberals generally claim that if one favors individual liberty one should place strong limitations on the activities of the state. Critics of liberalism often contest this implication by contesting the negative definition of liberty: they argue that the pursuit of liberty understood as self-realization or as self-determination (whether of the individual or of

the collectivity) can require state intervention of a kind not normally allowed by liberals. Many authors prefer to talk of positive and negative freedom. This is only a difference of style, and the terms 'liberty' and 'freedom' are normally used interchangeably by political and social philosophers. Although some attempts have been made to distinguish between liberty and freedom (Pitkin 1988; Williams 2001; Dworkin 2011), generally speaking these have not caught on. Neither can they be translated into other European languages, which contain only the one term, of either Latin or Germanic origin (e.g. liberté, Freiheit), where English contains both.

Safeguards of Liberty

Liberty is the most precious thing for an individual and effective steps are needed for its safeguards. From time immemorial there is tussle between the authority of the state and the liberties of the people. An individual enjoys more liberties if the authority of the state is curtailed. Byron says "Eternal vigilance is the price of liberty".

Liberty cannot exist in a dictatorial state. Prof. Laski points out certain steps for safeguarding liberty.

Firstly "Freedom will not be achieved for the mass of men pave under special guarantees" and it cannot "exist in the presence of privilege".

Secondly, "special privilege is incompatible with freedom".

Thirdly, "liberty cannot be realised in a state in which the rights of some depend upon the pleasures of others".

Fourthly, "state action is necessary for safeguarding liberty".

The following are some of the safeguards of liberty.

(1) Urge for liberty and vigilance :
The people in a state must have the urge for liberty and must be very vigilant to retain it.

(2) Democratic form of Government :
Democracy is a form of government where everybody has a share in administration. Only democratic governments can provide congenial atmosphere for the development of human personality. It is conducive for the full enjoyment of liberty.

(3) Separation of Powers :

Lord Acton opines that "Power corrupts an; absolute power corrupts absolutely." Power has a inner trend for misuse and power should act as a check to power.

The three branches of government: Executive, legislature and judiciary are to be separated although to Dr. Garner "absolute separation is neither possible nor desirable".

(4) List of fundamental Rights :

There must be a clear and unambiguous list of fundamental rights in the Constitution. The people must be conversant with their rights and the government must be aware of the limitation of powers. These rights are justiciable and any act that contravenes the provisions of the Constitution can be declared ultra vires.

(5) Independent Judiciary :

There must be an independent and impartial judiciary for the protection and preservation and individual liberty. The judiciary must be independent of executive and legislative control.

(6) Rule of Law :

The concept of Rule of law means all persons are equal before law. Law makes no distinction between the rich and poor, the high and low.

(7) Public opinion and free press :

Healthy public opinion and free press can do a lot to protect liberty. Free press can mobilise public opinion and will make people conscious and vigilant.

(8) Responsible Government :

A government formed by the representatives of the people is bound to be responsible. Any mistake on the part of the government will sound its death knell and the opposition party will capitalise on it. A bi-party system with a strong opposition will ensure necessary safeguard for liberty.

CHAPTER FOUR

EQUALITY

Equality is an important theme of normative political theory, which also is an important ideal of democracy. This lesson examines and explains the different senses in which the concept of equality is used.

Definition of Equality

Equality means, that whatever conditions are guaranteed to us, in the form of rights, shall also in the same measure be guaranteed to others, and that whatever rights are given to others shall also be given to us.

Equality like liberty is an important theme of democracy. Liberty and equality were understood to be one. Both the terms were considered to be of great importance since 19th century. Broadly speaking, equality implies a coherence of ideas that cover spheres ranging from man's search for the development of his personality in the society in which the strong and the weak live together, and both have the right of being heard.

Some Popular Definitions of Equality

1. The Right to Equality proper is a right of equal satisfaction of basic human needs, including the need to develop and use capacities which are specifically human. - D.D. Raphael

2. Equality means that no man shall be so placed in a society that he can over-reach his neighbour to the extent which constitutes a denial of latters citizenship. - Laski

3. Equality means equal rights for all the people and the abolition of all special rights and privileges. - Barker.

Dimension of Equality

Men are equal on their broad relationship in society. It is true that no government can equate dwarf to a tall man, and a stout to a lean man, but social institutions can extend to each individual, the status and the dignity of a human being. Viewed thus, the idea of equality has two side - positive and negative-that may be discussed as under:

Positive aspect of Equality

In a positive sense, equality means the provision of adequate opportunities to all, without any discrimination on the basis of birth, wealth, castle, colour, creed etc. No body should be debarred form certain facility just because of his status, caste, sex and creed.

Negative aspect of equality

It denotes, that, in its negative aspect, equality implies the absence of special privileges. There should be no artificial grounds of discrimination like those of religion, caste, colour, wealth, sex, etc, so that no talent should suffer from frustration for want of encouragement.

Kinds of Equality

There are different kinds of equality. They are:-

Natural Equality :

Natural equality rests on the principle that nature has created every one as equals. On the contrary, in reality we can seldom find such equality, as the world is prone with more inequalities than equality. People differ greatly in their intelligence, height, colour, physical strength and mental makeup. Natural equality is meant as the provision of equal treatment and equal opportunities to all human beings, irrespective of natural differences.

Civil Equality :

It implies of all before law. Irrespective of their status and position, all people should be treated equal and no discrimination should be made on the basis of caste, creed, sex, place of birth etc. Equal rights should be available to all the people and no body should be denied enjoyment of any right.

Political Equality :

Political equality is best guaranteed in a democracy. All citizens should have the right to participate in all affairs of the state without any discrimination on grounds of sex, race, religion, creed etc. Everything should be open to all people.

It means the enjoyment of political rights such as right to vote, right to contest in the election, right to hold public offices etc. It enables people's political participation and the principle of universal adult franchise is a manifestation of political equality.

Social Equality :

Social equality implies that no one should be regarded as high or low on the basis of his caste, colour, race or religion and no one person should be given special privileges on any of these consideration.

It stands for equality of status and absence of social barriers. It implies the abolition of social distinctions and strives for the establishment of class less society. In reality, there is no social equality as the Indian society is divided into different castes.

Economic Equality :

It means that there should be equal opportunity to all citizens in matters of availability of consumer goods, wealth and property. Similarly every on should have the same facility for jobs, work and in industry. There should be equal wages for equal work.

International Equality :

In means the principle of equality shall be extended to all people in all the countries. The same is true of nations and states. There cannot be different treatment between states and between peoples.

Relationship between Liberty and Equality

Liberty and Equality are closely related to each other. There is no value of liberty in the absence of equality. They are the same conditions viewed from different angles. They are the two sides of the same coin.

Though there is a close relationship between liberty and equality, yet there are some political thinkers who do not find any relationship between liberty and equality. For example, Lord Acton and De Tocqueville who were the ardent advocates of liberty, found no relationship between the two conditions.

To them liberty and equality were antagonistic and antithetical to each other. Lord Acton maintains that "The passion for equality made vain the hope for liberty". Such political thinkers maintain that where

there is liberty, there is no equality and vice versa. These political thinkers are of the opinion that people were conferred inequality by nature. We find inequality in nature also.

In some parts there are rivers while in others there are mountains and in still other parts there are plains and fields. No two persons are similar in their ability and capacity. And so there cannot be equality in society.

The views of Lord Acton and De Tocqueville are not accepted by modern political thinkers. Professor H.J. Laski has very aptly remarked in this connection: "To persons so ardent for liberty as Tocqueville and Lord Acton, liberty and equality, are antithetic things. It is a drastic conclusion. But it turns, in the case of both men, upon a misunderstanding of what equality implies".

These days, it is generally believed that liberty and equality should go together. If an individual is given unrestrained liberty to do whatever he likes, he will cause harm to others. There will be chaos in society if individuals are given unrestrained liberty.

In the nineteenth century, the Individualists wrongly interpreted the term 'Liberty'. They did not attach any importance to economic equality and laid stress on Laissez Faire to be adopted by the government. Adam Smith was the ardent advocate of this view.

The Individualists maintained that there should be a free competition between the capitalists and labour leaders. They did not want the government to interfere in the economic matters. Formula of Demand and Supply should be adopted. All the economic difficulties will be removed by this formula. If there will be excess of commodities and easy availability of labour, prices will come down. If there is scarcity, prices will rise higher and higher.

This formula was implemented in England and in many other countries of Europe and it resulted in dangerous consequences.

The government lost its control over the capitalists. The capitalists exploited the opportunity to the full. They exploited the labour to the full. As a result of it, the rich grew richer and poor became poorer. The
labour class suffered tragically.

As a result of it, an intense reaction took place against Individualism. This reaction led to the dawn of Socialism. Socialism condemned and refuted the principles of Individualism. Liberty has no significance in
the absence of economic equality. Professor Laski has very aptly remarked, "Where here are rich and poor, educated and uneducated, we always find a relation of master and servant".

C.E.M. Joad has also asserted, "The doctrine of liberty, of "which the importance cannot be over-estimated in politics, worked disastrously when applied in the field of economics".

Hobbes has also asserted, "What good is freedom to a starving man? He cannot eat freedom or drink it".

Thus, it is quite clear that economic equality is essential for the existence of political freedom. Otherwise it will be capitalist Democracy in which the labourers will have the right to vote but they will not be able to get their purposes served. Therefore, Liberty in the real sense of word is possible only in Socialistic democracy in which equality and liberty go together.

Similarly, it is also true that in the absence of political liberty, equality cannot be established. Mr. Elton True-blood has very aptly remarked in this connection. "The paradox is that equality and freedom, which

began by being ideas in conflict and tension, turn out open analysis to be necessary to each other. The truth is that it is impossible to make a reasonable statement of the meaning of equality except in terms of freedom. Men are equal only because all men are intrinsically free, as nothing else in all creation is free".

"Equality, in all its forms, must always be," says Barker, "subject and instrumental to the free development of capacity, but if it be pressed to the length of uniformity and if uniformity be made to thwart the free development of capacity, the subject becomes the master and the world is turned topsy-turvy".

R.H. Tawney has rightly remarked, "A large measure of equality, so far from being inimical to liberty, is essential to it".

Pollard also writes, "There is only one solution of the problem of liberty. It lies in equality". Thus, Liberty and Equality are complementary to each other. They are not opposed to each other. They go together. Liberty and Equality "are to be reconciled by remembering that both (liberty and equality) are subordinate means to the end of realising the potentialities of individual personality on the widest possible scale. The development of a rich variety of potentialities requires a large measure of liberty and forbids all attempts to impose a dead level of social and economic equality".

"There is an intimate connection between the two because all individual liberties are related to the basic equality of all men and because historically the aspiration for liberty became in practice and destruction of privilege or inequality".

Both are complementary to each other. "Liberty thus implies equality," says Herbert A. Dean, "liberty and equality are not in conflict nor even separate but are different facts of the same ideal ... indeed since they are identical, there can be no problem how or to what extent they are or can be related; this surely the nearest, if not the most satisfactory solution ever devised for a perennial problem in political philosophy".

CHAPTER FIVE

JUSTICE

Justice is the most important and most discussed objective of the State and Society. It is the basis of orderly human living. Justice demands the regulation of selfish actions of people for securing a fair distribution, equal treatment of equals and proportionate and just rewards for all. It stands for harmony between individual interests and the interests of society.

Justice is of central importance to political theory. In defending or opposing laws, policies, decisions and actions of government, appeals are made in the name of justice. Persons involved in every agitation for securing their interests always raise the slogan: "We want Justice". All civil rights movements are essentially movements for justice.

Justice stands for rule of law, absence of arbitrariness and a system of equal rights, freedoms and opportunities for all in society. In fact, Justice stands recognized as the first virtue or ideal or objective to be secured. In its Preamble, the Constitution of India gives first priority to the securing of social, economic and political justice for all its people. In contemporary times Justice stands conceptualized basically as Social Justice.

Justice: Meaning & Definition

Justice is a complex concept and touches almost every aspect of human life. The word Justice has been derived from the Latin word Jungere meaning 'to bind or to tie together'. The word 'Jus' also means 'Tie' or 'Bond'. In this way, Justice can be defined as a system in which men are tied or joined in a close relationship. Justice seeks to harmonise different values and to organise upon it all human relations. As such, Justice means bonding or joining or organising people together into a right or fair order of relationships.

Some popular definitions of Justice:

"Justice means to distribute the due share to everybody." - Salmond

"Justice protects the rights of the individual as well as the order of society." - Dr. Raphael

"Justice consists in a system of understandings and a procedure through which each is accorded what is agreed upon as fair." - C.E. Merriam

In other words, Justice means securing and protecting of rights of all in a fair way. It stands for harmony among all the people, orderly living and securing of rights of all in a just and fair way.

Key Features of Justice

1. Justice is related to mutual relationships of persons living in society.

2. Justice is based on values and traditions of society.

3. Justice is related to all aspects of human behaviour in society. Laws are made and courts are set up with this aim in view.

4. Aim of Justice is to provide equal rights, opportunities and facilities to all in a fair way.

5. The function of Justice is to harmonise individual interests with the interests of society.

6. Justices is a primary value and it is inseparably related to other values like Liberty, Equality and Property.

7. Justice is the principle of balancing or reconciling human relations in society in such a way as enables each one to get his due rights, towards and punishments.

8. Justice has several dimensions: Social Justice, Economic Justice, Political Justice and Legal Justice.

Types of Justice

1. Social Justice:

In contemporary times, a large number of scholars use prefer to describe the concept of Justice as Social Justice. Social Justice is taken to mean that all the people in a society are to be equal and there is to be no discrimination on the basis of religion, caste, creed, colour, sex or status.

However, various scholars explain the concept of Social Justice in different ways. Some hold that social justice is to allot to each individual his or her due share in the social sphere. According to some others, distribution of social facilities and rights on the basis of law and justice constitutes social justice.

What is Social Justice?

"Social justice is another name for equal social rights."

"Social Justice aims to provide equal opportunities to every individual to develop his inherent qualities." - Barker

"By social justice we mean ending all kinds of social inequalities and then to provide equal opportunities to everyone." - C.J.P.B. Gajendragadkar

Social democrats and modern liberal thinkers define social justice as the attempt to reconstruct the social order in accordance with moral principles. Attempts are to be continuously made to rectify social injustice. It also stands for a morally just and defensible system of distribution of reward and obligations in society without any discrimination or injustice against any person or class of persons.

In the Indian Constitution, several provisions have been provided with a view to secure social, economic and political justice. Untouchability has been constitutionally abolished. Every citizen has been granted an equal right of access to any public place, place of worship and use of places of entertainment.

The state cannot discriminate between citizens on the basis of birth, caste, colour, creed, sex, faith or title or status or any of these. Untouchability and apartheid are against the spirit of social justice. Absence of privileged classes in society is an essential attribute of social justice.

2. Economic Justice:

Economic Justice is indeed closely related to social justice because economic system is always an integral part of the social system. Economic rights and opportunities available to an individual are always a part of the entire social system.

Economic justice demands that all citizens should have adequate opportunities to earn their livelihood and get fair wages as can enable they to satisfy their basic needs and help them to develop further. The state should provide them economic security during illness, old age and in the event of a disability.

No person or group or class should be in a position to exploit others, nor get exploited. There should be fair and equitable distribution of wealth and resources among all the people. The gap between the rich and the poor should not be glaring. The fruits of prosperity must reach all the people.

There are present several different views regarding the meaning of economic justice. The liberals consider open competition as just and they support private property. On the other hand, the socialists seek to establish complete control of society upon the entire economic system.

They oppose private property. Whatever be the ideology or the system, one thing is clear and that is that all citizens must be provided with basic necessities of life. All citizens must have their basic needs of life fulfilled (Food, clothing, shelter, education, health and so on).

3. Political Justice:

Political justice means giving equal political rights and opportunities to all citizens to take part in the administration of the country. Citizens should have the right to vote without any discrimination on the basis of religion, colour, caste, creed, sex, birth or status. Every citizen should have an equal right to vote and to contest elections.

4. Legal Justice:

Legal justice has two dimensions - the formulation of just laws and then to do justice according to the laws. While making laws, the will of the rulers is not to be imposed upon the ruled. Laws should be based on public opinion and public needs. Social values, morality, conventions, the idea of just and unjust must be always kept in view.

When the laws do not meet the social values and rules of morality, citizens neither really accept nor abide by laws. In this situation, the enforcement of laws becomes a problem. Laws are just only when these are accepted not out of fear of external power but when inspired by internal feeling for the laws being good, just and reasonable.

Legal Justice means rule of law and not rule of any person. It includes two things: that all men are equal before law, and that law is equally applicable to all. It provides legal security to all. Law does not discriminate between the rich and the poor. Objective and due dispensation of justice by the courts of law is an essential ingredient of legal justice.

The legal procedure has to be simple, quick, fair, inexpensive and efficient. There should be effective machinery for preventing unlawful actions. "The aim of law is the establishment of what is legitimate; provide legal security and prevention of unjust actions." - Salmond.

Thus, Justice has four major dimensions: Social Justice, Economic Justice, Political Justice and Legal Justice. All these forms are totally inter-related and interdependent. Justice is real only when it exists in all these four dimensions. Without Social and Economic Justice, there can be no real Political and Legal Justice.

Presence of social and economic inequalities always leads to a denial of political and equal justice. An oppressed and poor person is virtually unable to participate is the political process or to seek the protection of law and law courts. Likewise, without political rights and equal protection of law no person can really get his social and economic rights and freedoms protected. Further, Justice needs the presence of rights, liberty and equality in society and only then can it really characterise life in society.

Theory of Justice

The question of justice has been central to every society, and in every age, it surrounds itself with debate. Justice has been the most critical part of a person's morality since time immemorial. Perhaps, it is for this reason that Plato, the ancient Greek philosopher, considered it crucial to reach a theory of justice.

Finding out the principles of justice is the main concern in Plato's Republic, to the extent that it is also subtitled as 'Concerning Justice'.

Ethics and Justice

In the Greek tradition of philosophy, political science was formulated after ethics. Ethics is referred to as a branch of learning that associates itself with good conduct. Ethics is, thus, that branch of philosophy that studies morality and deals with the questions of right and wrong.

The Greeks have considered ethics to be the foundations of Politics and Justice. According to Greek philosophy, the state comes into existence for the sake of life and continues for the sake of a good life, which makes it essential to have a "just society and a just state."

Plato, who can also be called the pioneer of Western Political Thought, viewed justice as a central question when dealing with politics (here, politics denote the subject of political science).

Plato and his thoughts

Greek political thought originates from Socrates. Plato was one of the most brilliant disciples of Socrates. Plato is considered the pioneer of Western Political thought today. It is because his mentor, Socrates, did not produce any writing, and we know of his thoughts only from the writings of Plato.

Plato, whose original name is Aristocles, was interested in pursuing philosophy and searching for the "truth". After the tragic death of Socrates, Plato produced various works on questions of State, Law, Justice, Politics and Philosophy. The Republic, in particular, is one of his most famous works. It deals with a wide range of ideas, and many of those ideas are relevant and are studied to date. Theory of Justice in Plato's Republic is worth studying for any political science student today.

Plato's Theory of Justice

Since the tradition of Greek Philosophy considered ethics to be important, they believed that the state comes into existence for the sake of life and continues for the sake of a good life. Plato believed in the same dictum and held that the state exists to fulfil the necessities of human life. The origin of the state, therefore, owed its existence to the fulfilment of human needs, and the Greek philosophers saw society and state as the same.

Unlike other living beings, human beings do not merely seek survival but essentially want to live a good life. Justice is the essential requirement to lead a good life. One cannot lead a good life without meeting their needs, and it's possible to meet one's needs only in the presence of Justice.

The Republic discusses Justice in the form of a dialogue. This methodology is known as Dialectical Method, which Plato borrowed from his mentor, Socrates. The dialogue takes place between Socrates, Glaucon, Adeimantus, Cephalus and Thrasymachus. The dialogue concluded that if one were allowed to suppress another, there would be complete anarchy, and it would be difficult to have any state of affairs. To save oneself from any such suffering and to prevent injustice, men enter into a contract to prevent injustice upon themselves or on others. That is also how laws came into existence to codify standard human conduct and bring a sense of Justice.

Essence of Justice

Socrates clarifies that justice is a relationship. A relationship among individuals relies on the kind of social organisation they inhabit. He further explains that justice can be analysed on a large scale, that is, state and then, on the level of the individual. Therefore, Plato's idea of justice believes that just individuals and just society are interwoven. To further understand Plato's theory of justice and its essence, it is important first to solve the issue of selecting the best ruler for the state. According to his argument, statesmanship is a special function and can only be performed by qualified persons with a moral character.

Then, in order to comprehend the nature of the state, the nature of man has to be understood too. Plato believed in "Like Man, Like State", implying that the character of the state is dependent on the character of its citizens. It also meant that once the nature of human beings is understood, it's easier to understand the functions of human society, and to arrive at the conclusion as to who is the best fit for ruling in this society.

Plato characterises human behaviour in three main sources:

Desire (or Appetite)

Emotion (or Spirit)

Knowledge (or Intellect)

Each human being has all three emotions but what varies is the degree to which these emotions are present in them. According to Plato, the ones who are restless and rapacious are fit for trade. Others who are driven by their emotion or spirit are best suited to become soldiers. Lastly, there are few who find no pleasure in worldly pursuits or victory and are satisfied in mediation. Such beings yearn to learn, and they are always in search of truth, and according to Plato, only these men of wisdom are fit to rule.

Plato thinks that just like the perfect individual is the one who has the ideal combination of desire, emotion and knowledge, a just state is the one that has individuals as its citizens for trade, to be soldiers and to rule. In the perfect state, individuals driven by desire will lead to growth and production but would not rule; the military armies would maintain security but not rule either. Only the individuals who have no appetite to gain material possession or power and are forces of knowledge would become the rulers.

Justice: the virtue of state

In his idea of justice, Plato identifies virtues that suit each social class.

The social class of traders, whose dominant trait is desire, the befitting virtue of traders is TEMPERANCE.

The social class of soldiers, whose dominant trait is spirit or emotion, the befitting virtue of soldiers is COURAGE.

The social class of Philosophers, whose dominant trait is knowledge or intellect, the befitting virtue of Philosophers is WISDOM.

The virtue that befits the state is JUSTICE which creates harmony in all the three social classes and is a necessary condition for human happiness.

The first three virtues belong to the respective three social classes, but the fourth virtue is a manifestation of harmony between all the three classes. These four virtues are also referred to as the four Cardinal Virtues of Plato's theory of Justice.

Philosopher-Kings: the cornerstone of Plato's theory of Justice

Plato is known for his unique concept of the philosopher-kings put forward in his political thought. He prescribed that the reins of government should remain with a very small class of philosopher-kings who represent REASON.

According to 'The story of Philosophy' by Will Durant, "the industrial forces would produce, but they would not rule, the military forces would protest, but they would not rule, the forces of knowledge and science and philosophy would be nourished and protected, and they would rule".

Plato's theory of Justice is famously known as the Architectonic Theory of Justice. He explains that as during the construction of a building, each part is assigned to different artisans, but the architect combines it to contribute to the final outlay of the building and add to its splendour. Similarly, the three cardinal virtues, namely Temperance, Courage and Wisdom would be cultivated by

Traders, Soldiers and Philosopher class respectively, and Justice, the fourth virtue, would act as the architect establishing a perfect state. Due to this inference between architecture and the organisation of society, his theory is also called the Architectonic Theory of Justice.

To conclude, Plato considers Justice to be a necessary condition of the good life. It is conducive to human happiness. The Republic, his famous work, is the most important work that explains his idea of justice. His theory of justice, built on moral foundations, with a clarification of virtues and classification of social classes, is considered today as relevant for all ages.

Difference between Platonic Justice and Modern Justice

(i) Platonic Justice is the moral concept of justice.

On the other hand, modern justice is legalistic. The courts provide justice on the basis of law.

(ii) Plato has formulated a concept of justice based on functional specialization.

But modern concept of justice has nothing to do with functional specialization.

(iii) Plato's concept of justice lays the foundation for fascism.

But in modern concept of justice, the idea of concentration of all powers to the state with reduction of freedom of individual is not encouraged.

(iv) According to the Platonic concept of justice, the philosopher king and the soldiers are to be placed above law.

But on the other hand, in modern concept of justice, everyone in the society, both the rulers and subjects are subjected to law.

(v) Plato's concept of justice is extremely passive being primarily individual and moral. It cannot be the basis of an active juristic interpretation. Accordingly, the critics are of the view that Plato's concept of justice is inapplicable in the context of the modern state.

Relationship between Justice, Liberty and Equality

Justice

The Preamble speaks of social, economic and political justice. The concept of justice goes beyond its narrow legal connotation. Significantly the words 'social' and 'economic' occur before the word 'political'.

Social justice implies that discrimination on the basis of birth, caste, race, sex or religion should cease. To that end, all citizens should enjoy equal opportunities in the matter of public appointment. It is the good of all people that the Government must strive to achieve. The concept of a welfare state as envisaged in the Directive Principles is an embodiment of guidelines for ensuring the social justice expected in the Preamble.

Economic justice implies that the gap between the rich and the poor is bridged, and the exploitation ceases. Removal of poverty is to be achieved not by taking away assets from those who have but by ensuring a more equitable distribution of national wealth and resources among those who contribute to its creation.

Thus the Directive Principles call upon the state to try and secure ownership and control over resources to subserve the common good, reduce the concentration of wealth, ensure equal pay for equal work, and see that people, especially women and children, are not abused or forced by economic want into work unsuitable for their age or strength.

Political justice implies that all citizens should have an equal opportunity to participate in the political system. One person-one vote is ensured irrespective not only of caste, sex or religion but also of proprietary or educational qualifications. It is the basis of the political democracy envisaged in the Constitution.

Liberty

Democracy is closely connected with the idea of liberty; certain minimal rights must be enjoyed by every person in a community for a free and civilized existence. These basic rights are spelt out by the Preamble as freedom of thought, expression, belief, faith and worship. The chapter on Fundamental Rights guarantees this freedom explicitly, subject to certain regulations; after all, liberty is not to degenerate into licence if democracy is to survive.

Equality

Rights have no meaning if they cannot be enjoyed equally by all members of the community. To ensure that it is possible for all to enjoy these rights, social and economic equality is sought to be achieved. The Fundamental Rights enjoin the State not to discriminate between citizen and citizen simply on the basis of caste, race, sex or religion. Public places are open to all citizens, titles of honour stand abolished, untouchability is abolished, among other things. The rule of law is to prevail: all citizens are equal before the law and enjoy equal protection of the laws of the land. Political equality is provided by the principle of universal adult franchise and by allowing, at least in principle, any citizen the opportunity to participate in the process of governance. Economically, the same ability and work entitle persons to the same salary.

The exploitation of an individual or group is to be removed.

CHAPTER SIX

RIGHTS

Rights are those essential conditions of social life without which no person can generally realize his best self. These are the essential conditions for health of both the individual and his society. It is only when people get and enjoy rights that they can develop their personalities and contributes their best services to the society.

Rights: Meaning and Definition

In simple words, rights are the common claims of people which every civilized society recognizes as essential claims for their development, and which are therefore enforced by the state.

1. "Rights are those conditions of social life without which no man can seek in general, to be himself at his best." - Laski

2. "Rights are powers necessary for the fulfillment of man's vocation as a moral being." - T. H. Green

3. "Rights are nothing more nor less than those social conditions which are necessary or favourable to the

development of personality." - Beni Prasad

As such, Rights are common and recognized claims of the people which are essential for their development as human beings.

Features/Nature of Rights

1. Rights exist only in society. These are the products of social living.

2. Rights are claims of the individuals for their development in society.

3. Rights are recognized by the society as common claims of all the people.

4. Rights are rational and moral claims that the people make on their society.

5. Since rights in here only in society, these cannot be exercised against the society.

6. Rights are to be exercised by the people for their development which really means their development in society by the promotion of social good. Rights can never be exercised against social good.

7. Rights are equally available to all the people.

8. The contents of rights keep on changing with the passage of time.

9. Rights are not absolute. These always bear limitations deemed essential for maintaining public health, security, order and morality.

10. Rights are inseparably related with duties. There is a close relationship between them. "No Duties No Rights. No Rights No Duties." "If I have rights it is my duty to respect the rights others in society".

11. Rights need enforcement and only then these can be really used by the people. These are protected and enforced by the laws of the state. It is the duty of a state to protect the rights of the people.

All these features clearly bring out the nature of Rights.

Types of Rights

1. Natural Rights:

Faith in natural rights is strongly expressed by several scholars. They hold that people inherit several rights from nature. Before they came to live in society and state, they used to live in a state of nature. In it, they enjoyed certain natural rights, like the right to life, right to liberty and right to property. Natural rights are parts of human nature and reason.

However, several other scholars regard the concept of natural rights as imaginary. Rights are the products of social living. These can be used only in a society. Rights have behind them the recognition of society as common claims for development, and that is why the state protects these rights.

2. Moral Rights:

Moral Rights are those rights which are based on human consciousness. They are backed by moral force of human mind. These are based on human sense of goodness and justice. These are not backed by the force of law. Sense of goodness and public opinion are the sanctions behind moral rights.

If any person violates any moral right, no legal action can be taken against him. The state does not enforce these rights. Its courts do not recognize these rights. Moral Rights include rules of good conduct, courtesy and of moral behaviour. These stand for moral perfection of the people Legal Rights.

Legal rights are those rights which are recognized and enforced by the state. Any violation of any legal right is punished by law. Law courts of the state enforce legal rights. These rights can be enforced against individuals and also against the government. In this way, legal rights are different from moral rights. Legal rights are equally available to all the citizens. All citizens enjoy legal rights without any discrimination. They can go to the courts for getting their legal rights enforced.

Legal Rights are of three types:

1. Civil Rights:

Civil rights are those rights which provide opportunity to each person to lead a civilized social life. These fulfill basic needs of human life in society. Right to life, liberty and equality are civil rights. Civil rights are protected by the state.

2. Political Rights:

Political rights are those rights by virtue of which citizens get a share in the political process. These enable them to take an active part in the political process. These rights include right to vote, right to get elected, right to hold public office and right to criticise and oppose the government. Political rights are really available to the people in a democratic state.

3. Economic Rights:

Economic rights are those rights which provide economic security to the people. These enable all citizens to make proper use of their civil and political rights. The basic needs of every person are related to his food, clothing, shelter, medical treatment etc. Without the fulfillment of these no person can really enjoy his civil and political rights. It is therefore essential, that every person must get the right to work, right to adequate wages, right to leisure and rest, and right to social security in case of illness, physical disability and old age.

Safeguards of Rights

1. Guarantee of Constitution:

Fundamental rights of the people in every stale are guaranteed by the constitution which ensures to the citizens the enjoyment of their rights free from any interference.

But the declaration of rights by the constitution does not necessarily guarantee the enjoyment of rights.

2. Independence of the Judiciary:

The rights of the people can be safeguarded only by an impartial and independent judiciary.

3. Rule of Law:

It implies the equality of everybody, rich or poor, high or low in the eyes of law.

4. Separation of Powers:

According to Montesquieu and Black- stone, the combination of executive, legislative and judicial powers in a person or set of persons might result in the loss of individual liberty.

But a rigid separation of powers is neither desirable nor practicable.

5. Democracy:

It is the only form of government in which people can have the opportunity to protect their rights.

6. Absence of Special Privileges:

Liberty is the common and equal possession of all and it cannot be enjoyed by all the people, when certain people enjoy some special privileges.

CHAPTER SEVEN

GENDER

Introduction

Gender has increasingly been acknowledged as an important variable in analyses and development planning. In recent years, the goals of equality, justice and peace in human development have been adopted by the WID (Women and Development) approach and Sustainable Development Goals which aim to eliminate all forms of discrimination and violence against women in public and private spheres. Gender equality today is not only a fundamental human right but a necessary foundation for a peaceful and sustainable world. Equal access to education, health, decent work, representation in political and economic decision making process are not only rights that women should have ,they also benefit the humanity at large. However, studies reveal that the subject of gender inequality is deep rooted in almost all societies, women constitute a half of the human race and are subject to discrimination and subordination in the sphere of education, employment, land rights ,food and nutrition.

Much academic research on North East India has tended to look at the region as homogenous from the perspective of gender and gender relations, thereby ignoring the diversity in gender related issues. But studies have revealed that women in the North East have been marginalized on various issues of which relations of rights and power have been matters of concern to social scientists. Feminist research have often focused on the need to raise the issue of women's exclusion from the power structure but the fact remains that power is still very much male centric. Even in matrilineal societies like that of the Khasi , Jaintia and Garo, women areexcluded from the decision- making process. Besides power relations, other spheres of subordination of women in the North East have been in the area of resource distribution and security over resources like land ,economy, livelihood etc. Literacy and education ,which are the most important indicators of social development also reveal disparity between the sexes.Still another matter of serious concern is the discrimination of women in the economic sector and commodification in the new era of globalization.

Gender refers to the socially constructed roles of and relations between men and women. It implies the social qualities and opportunities involved with being male and female. It also refers to the relationship between women and men and girls and boys, as well as the relations between women and those between men. Gender is a cultural term. It refers to the different roles which the society, assigns to men and women. It distinguishes between 'masculine' and 'feminine' stereotypes. The concept of gender was become popular in the early lifes in the field of feminism, sociology and psychology.

On the other hand, Sex refers to the biological and physiological differences between men and women. The term sex is a physical differentiation between the biological male and thefemale. The infant is identified as a boy or a girl depending on his or her sex. It refers to biological factors which distinguish man from woman. Judith Butler says "Sex is not just an analytical category. It is a normative category as well. It stipulated what men and women are. It also stipulates what men and women ought to be. It formulates rules to regulate the behaviour of men and women.

Distinguishing between sex and gender is nothing but a debate of nurture our nature. Sex refers to the biological differences between men and women and gender indicates the vast range of cultural meanings attached to that basic difference. The distinction between sex and gender was first emerged in the 1950s and 1960s in the writings of British and American psychiatrists and medical personnel engaged to cure intersex and trans-sexual patients. To distinguish between the two Simon de Beauvoir rightly says "women are made, they are not born". It indicates the cultural aspects of sex.

Definitions of Gender

Gender refers to the characteristics of women, men, girls and boys that are socially constructed. This includes norms, behaviours and roles associated with being a woman, man, girl or boy, as well as relationships with each other. As a social construct, gender varies from society to society and can change over time. - World Health Organisation

Merriam-Webster Dictionary defines Gender as a subclass within a grammatical class (such as noun, pronoun, adjective or verb) of a language that is partly arbitrary but also partly based on distinguishable characteristics (such as shape, social rank, manner of existence or sex) and that determines agreement with and selection of other words or grammatical forms.

Oxford Dictionary defines Gender as the fact of being male or female, especially when considered with reference to social and cultural differences, rather than differences in biology; members of a particular gender as a group.

Gender as Legal Status

In European societies, Roman law, post-classical canon law and later common law, referred to a person's sex as male, female or hermaphrodite, with legal rights as male or female depending on the characteristics that appeared most dominant. Under Roman law, a hermaphrodite had to be classed as either male or female. The 12th-century Decretum Gratiani states that "Whether an hermaphrodite may witness a testament, depends on which sex prevails". The foundation of common law, the 16th Century Institutes of the Lawes of England, described how a hermaphrodite could inherit "either as male or female, according to that kind of sexe which doth prevaile." Legal cases where legal sex was placed in doubt have been described over the centuries.

In 1930, Lili Elbe received emasculation and ovary transplant and changed her legal gender as female. In 1931, Dora Richter received removal of the penis and vaginoplasty. A few weeks after Lili Elbe had her final surgery including uterus transplant and vaginoplasty. Immune rejection from transplated uterus caused her death. In May 1933, Institute for Sexual Research was attacked by Nazi and there are no record about Richter after this attack.

After World War II, transgender issues received public attention again. Christine Jorgensen was unable to marry man because her birth certificate listed her as male. Some transsexuals changed their birth certificates, but its validity were challenged. In United Kingdom, Sir Ewan Forbes, 11th Baronet case recognized legal gender change of intersex person. However legal gender change of transsexuals were not recognized in Corbett v Corbett.

Nowadays, many jurisdictions allow transgender individuals to change their legal gender. However there are some obstacles. Some jurifications require sterilization, childlessness or unmarried status for legal gender change.

In some cases, legal gender of transsexual's who did not revised public documents yet become problems. In some cases, courts accept their gender identity if they received sex reassignment surgery.

Growing intersex awareness movements or non-binary movements caused legal recognition of non-binary gender for some jurisdictions.

The Sociological Understanding of Gender

The sociology of gender is a subfield of sociology which concerns itself with masculinity and femininity i.e. social construction of gender, how gender interacts with other social forces and relates to the overall social structure. The field of study under gender sociology diversified over the years and has incorporated the feminist viewpoint. The starting point in the field is sex/gender distinction.

Sex/Gender Distinction

Sex and gender are used interchangeably in everyday life to refer to whether someone is male or female. However, in the 1970s, the feminist school of thought drew a clear distinction between the two. Sex is a biological construct which determines whether an individual is male or female based on a number of biological markers such as reproductive organs, hormones, chromosomes, external genitalia, etc. However, not all individuals have all their biological markers aligned to fit a certain sex on the male/female binary. Such people whose organs do not align with either category are called intersex. Gender is a social construct which reflects the social expectation of expression of one's identity, presentation of self-behaviour and interaction with others. It is a social category which reflects learned behaviour and culturally produced identity.

The terms sex and gender are often used interchangeably. However, in a discussion of gender socialization, it's important to distinguish between the two.

Sex is biologically and physiologically determined based on an individual's anatomy at birth. It is typically binary, meaning that one's sex is either male or female.

Gender is a social construct. An individual's gender is their social identity resulting from their culture's conceptions of masculinity and femininity. Gender exists on a continuum.

Individuals develop their own gender identity, influenced in part by the process of gender socialization.

Social Construction of Gender

As famously stated by Simone de Beauvoir, "One is not born but rather becomes a woman". Gender as one of the basic structures of human society is taught to kids through socialization at an early age. Parents are the biggest influence in the socialization of a child since they reinforce societal rules and gender norms by rewarding gender-appropriate behaviour and punishing any deviations. By the age of 3, all children develop a concrete idea of gender identity which remains mostly constant for the rest of their lives. This leads to the creation of gender roles. The term 'gender role' coined by John Money in a 1955 paper where he defined it as, "all those things that a person says or does to disclose himself or herself as having the status of a boy or man, girl or woman". These gender roles are so ingrained in mindsets that they are not consciously enforced rather unconsciously imposed on children. From the pink/blue binary to the choice of dolls for girls and guns and cars for boys as toys, gender socialization is everywhere. Even language is gender influenced. While girls are complimented as pretty and beautiful, boys are complimented as smart and brave. These reinforce the ideal qualities that these individuals grow up to prioritize.

Author Susan Grieshaberin in "Constructing the Gendered Infant" suggested that attitudes regarding pregnancy change once parents find out the sex of their child. According to her, parents start planning the child's arrival keeping the child's gender in mind. Thus the world that the child enters is already gendered for that child to conform to.

Masculinity and Femininity

Feminist scholarship has largely focused on women's experience with femininity to highlight the oppression and power hierarchies that they face because of their gender. However, Connell (1987) gave the first systematic research analysis of both sets of constructions in the form of "hegemonic masculinity and emphasized femininity" and how they contribute to global gender inequality. "Hegemonic Masculinity" is oriented towards accommodating the interest and desires of men and thus forms the basis of patriarchal social order. She argued that there are many masculinities that operate and while all masculinities are privileged over all femininities, there is a certain idea of masculinity which holds greater gender power and is thus hegemonic. This gender power is held by white, middle class, highly educated, able-bodied, heterosexual men. Masculinity is policed so that there is conformity to the social construct. Insults such as "You are a Fag" (derogatory word for homosexuals) or "Don't cry like a girl" while on one hand reinforce the patriarchal idea of masculinity but also simultaneously ingrain the idea other genders and sexualities are inferior and thus the comparison to them is an insult.

Feminist author Nivedita Menon states genders are performed which means that no one can prove that they are masculine and then rest assured in the belief that their gender has been sufficiently established and proved. They need to conform to the same roles and perform them every day to reinforce their gender constantly. For example, even the most well-built, moustached, tall, muscular guy (ideal body stereotypes for men) cannot wear a saree to work because non-conformity to gender roles even for a day can cause a backlash.

"Emphasised Femininity" is defined around compliance with female subordination and is oriented to accommodating the interest and desires of men. Women are taught to view marriage as an important life goal. Media and pop culture constantly reinforce the need for women to adjust in marriages to make them successful. Working women suffer "mother's guilt" for prioritizing their careers over their children. Feminist scholars have used the social construction of femininities to explain wage inequality, the global "feminization of poverty" and women's relegation to "feminine" labour markets (example: secretarial labour, garment industry, caring labour) and to the so-called private realm of household and family.

Critiquing the Sex/Gender Binary

Feminists came up with sex/gender distinction to counter biological determinism. However, sex/gender distinction has its own flaws. First is the Particularity argument given by Elizabeth Spelman (1988). She argued that sex/gender distinction reinforces gender realism which is the idea that one common thread unites people of one gender. For example, sexual objectification is faced by all women according to MacKinnon's view. So all women experience womanhood in the same way irrespective of race, class, ethnicity, etc. This allows for white, middle class, feminist perspectives of womanhood to be passed on as the litmus test for whether someone is truly a woman or not. The second is the Normativity argument by Judith Butler (1999) who states that the current definition of a woman is not wrong rather there should be no definition at all. In an attempt to define women against the biologically deterministic ideas, feminists have created new boxes for women to fit in. That the definition of the term woman is supposedly fixed "operates as a policing force which generates and legitimises certain practices, experiences, etc. and curtails and delegitimises others (Nicholson, 1998). Besides the idea of a fixed biological binary sex has been debunked. Sex itself is believed to be a social construct and many of the differences observed in male and female bodies that were earlier attributed to sex have come to be seen as a result of social upbringing. Thus fourth-wave feminism is increasingly questioning the sex/gender binary.

Queer Theory

Once the term queer was associated with homosexuals and had a strong homophobic undertone. But the term has been reclaimed by the LGBTQIA + movement to refer to all individuals whose sexuality, gender identity, gender expression and bodies do not conform to dominant societal norms. Both feminism and queer theory are interdisciplinary studies that question the dominant understanding of gender by problematizing the relationship that exists between gender identity, anatomical sex and sexual orientation (Fineman, 2009). The queer movement worldwide has been arguing for gender fluidity and non-binary sexes to create a more inclusive, non-heteronormative world.

Transgender

The gender binary between male and female is a modern concept propagated by western science and imposed upon non-western cultures through colonization. Many cultures in pre colonized era not only recognized other genders but also deeply respected them. Gender fluidity is still the norm in many African cultures. Here we look at two such communities.

The Hijra community in India consisting of eunuchs, intersex and transgender people was recognized as the third gender along with the rest of the transgender community. However, the hijra community does not associate itself with the rest of the transgender community as it has a separate culture which has been passed down through generations by the 'gharanas'. Hijras have traditionally been associated with 'Ardhnareshwar', a form of Shiva and Parvati. They are believed to have divine connections with God since they are above the gender confines. They were considered to hold religious authority and were sought for blessings.

The Navajo Native American culture recognized two other genders known as the 'Two Spirits' which are the feminine man (nádleehí) and masculine woman (dilbaa).

They are considered to embody the masculine and feminine traits of their ancestors and nature. They are chosen to represent their culture and once chosen have to live their lives in their adopted gender. They can have sex with either gender and their children are adopted in the Two-Spirit household without any stigma.

Intersectionality

Kimberle Crenshaw, an American lawyer coined the term intersectionality in 1989 in her work, "Mapping the Margins: Intersectionality, Identity Politics and Violence Against Women of Colour". Intersectionality refers to overlapping social identities such as gender, race, class etc. which amplify discrimination. It is a recognition that even within minority groups, people face different levels of discrimination based on their other identity markers. While all women are oppressed by patriarchy, black women face more oppression than white women. Poor black women face more discrimination than rich black women and so on. While the concept originated in terms of gender study, it is widely used in sociology today to highlight all kinds of intersectional oppression across identities.

Major Sociological Theories

Structural Functionalism

The theory came about in the 20th century and has played a major role in gender studies. It assumes the family as the most integral part of society and explains gender roles in this context. Functionalists argue that gender roles were established well before the pre industrialised era where men primarily cater to the needs outside the house such as collecting food and women took care of the homes. This arrangement was functional because women were constrained by physical restraints of pregnancy and nursing and were unable to leave homes for long periods of time. These roles were passed on in subsequent generations. However, during WWII, many women assumed the role of the breadwinner as men went out for war. When men returned from the war and wanted to reclaim their jobs, society fell into imbalance as women refused to forfeit their wage-earning jobs.

Conflict Theory

According to the theory, the society is a struggle for dominance between competing groups where one group (the dominant group) dominates over other groups (the submissive groups). In gender studies, men form the dominant group while women are the submissive group. Social problems arise when the dominant group exploits and oppresses the subordinate groups. It is difficult for women to attain equal status in society since men as the dominant group make the rules for success, dominance and power in society.

Feminist Theory

Feminist Theory examines gender relations and power structures. It looks for ways in which gender roles are perpetuated in society and women as the subordinate group actively support the structure that perpetuates their oppression. Feminism especially radical feminism seeks to topple this structure termed patriarchy. Patriarchy is a system by which men (seen as the patriarch and head of the family) are given more power and their contributions more valued by virtue of their gender identity. This branch of gender theory is increasingly gaining more traction in gender sociology.

Symbolic Interactionism

Unlike other theories in sociology which use biological determinism to explain the differences in male and female behaviour, this theory suggests that humans behave in accordance with the symbolic significance of a certain concept. Simply stated, it refers to the social construction of gender and how men and women have different symbolic traits and expectations attached to them. Men are supposed to be more logical while women are supposed to be more emotional. So while dealing with other individuals, a person would try to be more logical or emotional based on whether the person he is interacting with is male or female. Thus gender difference comes out of 'doing gender roles'.

Gender Socialization

Gender socialization is the process by which we learn our culture's gender-related rules, norms and expectations. The most common agents of gender socialization — in other words, the people who influence the process — are parents, teachers, schools and the media. Through gender socialization, children begin to develop their own beliefs about gender and ultimately form their own gender identity.

Gender Socialization in Childhood

The process of gender socialization begins early in life. Children develop an understanding of gender categories at a young age. Studies have shown that children can discern male voices from female voices at six months old, and can differentiate between men and women in photographs at nine months old. Between 11 and 14 months, children develop the ability to associate sight and sound, matching male and female voices with photographs of men and women. By age three, children have formed their own gender identity. They have also begun to learn their culture's gender norms, including which toys, activities, behaviors and attitudes are associated with each gender.

Because gender categorization is a significant part of a child's social development, children tend to be especially attentive to same-gender models. When a child observes same-gender models consistently exhibit specific behaviors that differ from the behaviors of other-gender models, the child is more likely to exhibit the behaviors learned from the same-gender models. These models include parents, peers, teachers and figures in the media.

Children's knowledge of gender roles and stereotypes can impact their attitudes towards their own and other genders. Young children, in particular, may become especially rigid about what boys and girls "can" and "cannot" do. This either-or thinking about gender reaches its peak between the ages of 5 and 7 and then becomes more flexible.

Agents of Gender Socialization

As children, we develop gender-related beliefs and expectations through our observations of and interactions with the people around us. An "agent" of gender socialization is any person or group that plays a role in the childhood gender socialization process. The four primary agents of gender socialization are parents, teachers, peers and the media.

Parents

Parents are typically a child's first source of information about gender. Starting at birth, parents communicate different expectations to their children depending on their sex. For example, a son may engage in more roughhousing with his father, while a mother takes her daughter shopping. The child may learn from their parents that certain activities or toys correspond with a particular gender (think of a family that gives their son a truck and their daughter a doll). Even parents who emphasize gender equality may inadvertently reinforce some stereotypes due to their own gender socialization.

Teachers

Teachers and school administrators model gender roles and sometimes demonstrate gender stereotypes by responding to male and female students in different ways. For example, separating students by gender for activities or disciplining students differently depending on their gender may reinforce children's developing beliefs and assumptions.

Peers

Peer interactions also contribute to gender socialization. Children tend to play with same-gender peers. Through these interactions, they learn what their peers expect of them as boys or girls. These lessons may be direct, such as when a peer tells the child that a certain behavior is or is not "appropriate" for their gender. They can also be indirect, as the child observes same and other gendered peers' behavior over time. These comments and comparisons may become less overt over time, but adults continue to turn to same-gendered peers for information about how they are supposed to look and act as a man or a woman.

Media

Media, including movies, TV and books teaches children about what it means to be a boy or a girl. Media conveys information about the role of gender in people's lives and can reinforce gender stereotypes. For example, consider an animated film that depicts two female characters: a beautiful but passive heroine and an ugly but active villain. This media model and countless others, reinforces ideas about which behaviors are acceptable and valued (and which are not) for a particular gender.

Gender Socialization Throughout Life

Gender Socialization is a lifelong process. The beliefs about gender that we acquire in childhood can affect us throughout our lives. The impact of this socialization can be big (shaping what we believe we are capable of accomplishing and thus potentially determining our life's course), small (influencing the color we choose for our bedroom walls) or somewhere in the middle.

As adults, our beliefs about gender may grow more nuanced and flexible, but gender socialization can still affect our behavior, whether in school, the workplace or our relationships.

Gender in Political Theory

Like all concepts in political theory, gender has a history. Unlike most of these concepts, though the history of gender is comparatively short. The term itself originated in the nineteenth century, arising in the context of descriptive and diagnostic social sciences of human behaviour. It was only adopted into political theory, as a result of a political process of struggle, about 100 years later in the 1970s. When it arrived, gender was itself a highly political concept, signalling a rearrangement of the scope, terms and politics of political theory itself. Gender theorists at that point conceived of their work within political theory as a further engagement of feminism with 'malestream' thought, that is, theorisations of politics written by men and reflecting their assumptions and interests. The feminist stance towards the discipline and towards its traditionalist practitioners was critical and transformative.

To understand this important development in political theory, however we will need to examine the concepts of sex and sexuality as well. Moreover, it will also be necessary to bear in mind that gender, woman and women's lives are all feminist concepts, but that within feminism itself they are not all the same thing. Finally, to make matters even more interesting, political theory is now engaged with theorisations of gender drawn from very recent developments, such as cultural studies, media studies, multiculturalism, post-structuralism and post-modernisms. These ideas and interests are not necessarily aligned with all, or indeed any, of contemporary feminisms in terms of subject matter or inspiration. On the whole, though there is a tremendous debt in this area to feminist thought.

While strong claims can be made for understanding gender in feminist frame, this is to some extent a matter of acknowledging a conceptual development in history, rather than stating a necessary truth about the concept. Political theory itself records any number of historical encounters in which specific movements have defined and deployed philosophical concepts, which have then been dropped or redefined as political circumstances changed. 'Monarch', 'republic', 'citizen', 'equality', 'right' and 'obligation' are obvious examples. Gender is another concept in political theory recording and consolidating a political engagement, that of feminism with malestream thought, but its own conceptual genesis predates contemporary feminisms and its future is open to other interpretative moves and political movements.

Gender is arguably the biggest thing to hit political theory since democracy. Equally arguably, gender is a conceptualisation that has arisen within the globalised thrust of democratic political change. This movement has not only expanded the categories of persons deemed worthy to share in ruling and being ruled, it has also expanded the scope of state power to determine rights and obligations, to protect and regulate all kinds of activities and to promote and distribute material welfare. As mentioned above, the emancipation of women from restricted civil liberties and reduced material welfare is proceeding and this has brought considerations of sex (specifically as femaleness) into political theory from a new perspective. It has also raised corresponding issues concerning men, along with matters related to children and 'family' roles, including reproductive heterosexuality. This has effectively and irrevocably politicised an apparently natural order of things. Something of the same considerations apply to sexualities alternative to reproductive heterosexuality, further loosening the grip of naturalising accounts that validate behaviours for some and criminalise or demean the behaviours of others.

Concepts of sex and sexuality are linked to behaviour via theories of gender, of which I have outlined three. These do the additional work of raising a description or categorisation into an issue. Behavioural theories of gender map the distance between behaviours (both sexed and sexual) and the presumed fixities of reproductive biology or psychoanalytical development. Power theories of gender track the disparities of power and resources between behavioural groups (from masculine/heterosexual men on down) as society reproduces them through educational and disciplinary processes. Performative theories of gender present the binary and hierarchical character of the concepts through which the lived experience of sex and sexuality is constructed, including the supposed 'natural' truths of reproductive biology.

Performative theories of gender are most effective in linking gendered theory to further theories of 'difference', typically involving race/ethnicity, cultural markers and multiculturalism, religious and linguistic identities and so on. They have the effect of removing the claims of any one characteristic, even the bodily characteristics we demarcate as sex, from any clear prioritisation over any other characteristic. This defuses debates as to which identity, or which form of oppression or discrimination is more significant or hurtful or pressing, because that form of identity is more intrinsic, natural, unchangeable, inevitable or foundational to the human person. Prioritisation must come through a clearly political process and cannot, on this view, be factored into 'natural' hierarchies and binaries.

This move could facilitate an interesting rainbow of coalition politics and a clearer alignment of political theory with all sections of any given community than canonical texts have allowed. On the other hand, the extent to which more traditional and foundational conceptualisations of 'difference' have a more immediate appeal and thus a long-term future, is undeniable, given the way that political organisation and conceptual discussion tend to proceed along familiar, well-trodden paths, perhaps for very good reasons. Ultimately gender could dissolve into one aspect of the 'politics of difference' among others. Alternatively, the universality of sex and sexuality and their persistent connection to power relations in society suggest that the concept of gender will attain a permanent and salient position in the political theory of the future.

CHAPTER EIGHT

CITIZENSHIP

Introduction

In each and every countries of the world, we find Citizens as well as some Foreigners. Citizens are the permanent residents of a State. Foreigners are the temporary residents who resides in the form of diplomats, ambassadors, students, professionals, businessmen and tourists. They have settled in a foreign country with official authorization. Foreigners are the legal residents in a state along with the Citizens. They enjoys some rights which are granted some rights by the state in which they reside.

But the Illegal Alien or Illegal Immigrants are those who have infiltrated into the territory of other country illegally or without official authorization. They are against the interests of the State.

At present, some countries of the world are facing the problems of Illegal Alien like India, U.S. and so on. The North Eastern Region of India is facing a grave threat and challenges posed by the Illegal Aliens. In India, most of the Illegal Immigration of Aliens takes place from Bangladesh. The issue of Illegal Alien is found to be more in North

Eastern States of India in comparison to other parts of India and to the world as well.

The Assam Movement from 1979-85 is one of the best example of movement against such Illegal Aliens. The Indigenous People of Assam suspected that there were many Illegal Aliens from Bangladesh. They felt that unless those alien nationals are detected and deported, they would reduce the Indigenous People of Assam into a microscopic minority in their own lands.

Even though the Assam Movement ended with the signing of the historic Assam Accord on 15th August 1985, but it did not solve the problems of the Illegal Immigration. The issue of the Illegal Aliens still continues to be a burning issue in the politics of Assam.

The concept of Citizenship originated in the ancient Greek City States. The word citizen is derived from the word "City". Citizen generally means an inhabitant of a City. In the golden age of Pericles in the 5th century B.C., the Athenian citizenship had its climax. The credit of developing the idea of Citizenship goes to the people of Athens in the ancient times. The Athenians decided to enter into a life partnership with the State. They wanted this partnership for happiness, goodness and virtue (knowledge or wisdom). They also enjoyed several civil and political rights. The Athenian Citizens regarded themselves as superior to the non-citizens. During that time, women and slaves were regarded as the non-citizens. They were treated as commodities. We do not find the idea of Citizenship in clear terms in other countries in those days. That is why credit is given to Athens for developing the idea of Citizenship.

As a Citizen, each and everyone has some rights and duties towards his or her State. There is a close relationship between Citizenship and the political life of the individuals. Citizens constitute the indispensable parts of the State and the State exists for their welfare. The future of a State depends on the quality of its Citizens.

In the modern states of contemporary world, Good Citizenship has become very essential. It is an important quality of the State. The future of a State with Good Citizens is very bright. A democracy can be made successful only by Good Citizens. Good Citizenship is a political and social necessity. Some of the qualities of a Good Citizen are:-

a. The principal quality of a Good Citizen is his ability and desire to discharge duties.
b. The Citizens must be intelligent, alert and reasonable. Lord Bryce considers these qualities to be very important for Good Citizenship.
c. Political consciousness is another important quality of a Good Citizen. He must be vigilant about the social problems. If he is not conscious about the problems of the state, he cannot be considered as a Good Citizen.
d. A Good Citizen is one who is loyal to the State and its Constitution. He must abide by the laws of the State.
e. Another quality of Good Citizenship is a spirit of independence. He must be in a position to express his views freely.
f. To be a Good Citizen, one must pay his dues to the State properly and in time.

In the literal sense, a person who lives in a city is said to be a Citizen. But in the discipline of Political Science, we use this term in a different sense. To find the real meaning of the term, we are to go back to ancient Greece. Aristotle, the father of Political Science, called a person a Citizen, who would take a direct and active part in the administration of the State.

Since the States in the ancient Greece were as small as the cities of Greece, it was possible for the residents of the City State to make law, to adjudicate and even enforce the law.

Modern Nation States are geographically very large. Therefore some advanced countries of the world use the term Statizen. The word Statizen is a contemporary version of Citizen.

Foreigners

In each and every state of the world, we find some Foreigners. They reside temporarily as diplomats, professionals, businessmen, students or that they may be casual visitors or tourists. Though Foreigners owe loyalty to the State to which they belong, they have to obey the law of the State in which they stay temporarily. Modern democratic states have become very liberal towards Foreigners also, for example, a large number of Indians are living in foreign countries. They live in foreign countries as long as they like. These people enjoy most of the rights of those states. In the eye of law, they are Foreigners, but practically they may not feel like that because of the democratic atmosphere of a state. Now-a-days, most of the countries bear liberal attitude towards the Foreigners.

Difference Between Citizens and Foreigners

In every state, there are two classes of people – the Citizens and the Foreigners. The Citizens are the permanent residents of the State. They abide by the law of the State and owe allegiance to the State. Whereas, a Foreigner is one, who is a temporary resident of a State.

There are certain differences between the Citizens and the Foreigners living in a State. Some of them are mentioned below:-

a. The Citizens are the permanent residents of a State. But a Foreigner lives temporarily in a State. He goes back to his country when his job in a foreign state is over. But the Foreigners can also acquire the citizenship of this state according to law.
b. A Citizen is bound to discharge all types of duties towards the State. He may be asked even to sacrifice his life for the State. But a Foreigner cannot be compelled to do that. He gets all protection from the State of his temporary residence and is bound to obey its laws.

So in each and every countries of the world, we can find Citizens as well as some Foreigners. Foreigners are the legal residents in a State along with the Citizens. They have migrated from a foreign country with official authorization.

Aliens or Illegal Aliens

An Illegal Alien or Illegal Immigrant refers to those people who is living without official authorization in a country of which they are not a Citizen.

The Illegal Alien are those immigrants, who has entered in a foreign country in an unlawful way or without permission. Bangladeshis form the largest number of such Illegal Aliens in India. The Illegal Aliens however differ from the Foreigners. While Foreigners are those people who have migrated in a legal way like diplomats, ambassadors, businessmen, students and tourists; but the Illegal Aliens have infiltrated into the territory of other country without official authorization. However the number of Illegal Aliens in North East India are so large that they are posing a serious threat to the Indigenous People. There is no such other country in the world, who can bear such a huge number of the Illegal Aliens.

The Assam Movement from 1979-85 is one of the best example of movement against such Illegal Aliens. The Indigenous People of Assam suspected that there were many Illegal Immigrants from Bangladesh. They felt that unless those alien nationals are detected and deported, they would reduce the Indigenous People of Assam into a minority in their own lands.

Even though the Assam Movement was ended with the signing of the historic Assam Accord on 15th August 1985, but it did not solve the problems of the Illegal Aliens. The issue of the Illegal Aliens still continues to be a dominating issue in the politics of Assam.

Even though there are Illegal Aliens in other parts of India or other countries of the world as well, the number of Illegal Aliens in North East India is much higher. If the process of Illegal Immigration continues unchecked in North East India, the Indigenous People or the sons of the soil of North East India will soon be reduced to a microscopic minority in their own lands.

Definition of the term citizen

According to Aristotle, citizen is he "who has the power to take part in the deliberative or judicial administration of any state is said by us to be a citizen of that state".

Vattal has defined citizens as, "the members of a civil society bound to this society by certain duties, subject to its authority and equal participants in its advantages".

"Citizenship", according to Laski, "is the contribution of one's instructed judgment to the public good".

Aristotle's Views on Citizenship

For Aristotle the human is "by nature" destined to live in a political association. Yet not all who live in the political association are citizens, and not all citizens are given equal share in the power of association. The idea of Polity is that all citizens should take short turns at ruling. It is an inclusive form of government: everyone has a share of political power. Aristotle argues that citizen are those who are able to participate in the deliberative and judicial areas of government. However, not all who live in a political association are citizens. Women, children, slaves, and alien residents are not citizens. Some groups; the rich, the poor, those who come from noble families and the virtuous, can claim power in the state.

Polis exits by nature, and human beings are naturally

adapted to live in a Polis. Initially appears the family. Then several families amalgamate to form a village. When several villages amalgamate into a community large enough to be self-sufficient, they form a state, "Polis". Polis "comes to be for the sake of living, but it remains in existance for the sake of living well". According to Aristotle, studying the mature and fully developed specimen is the best way to understand the nature of being. To comprehend the nature of the thing one does not need to look to its origin but to its full development.

Every city-state exists by NATURE, since the first communities do. For the city-state is their end, and nature is an end; for we say that each thing's nature is the character it has when its coming-into-being has been completed.

According to Aristotle, citizen is he "who has the power to take part in the deliberative or judicial administration of any state is said by us to be a citizen of that state".

Artisans, trades persons, and those who do not own property are not given equal share in power of the state. They are not "citizens" in respect to ruling. Polity is "a mixture of oligarchy and democracy", is an attempt to combine the freedom of the poor majority and the wealth of the rich minority. Rule is a complex of activities that can be allocated to different social categories. Polity is the form of government in which different organs of government are controlled by different sections of the population, in such a way that both rich and poor have a share of power. Because power is shared by all categories, all take turns to rule.

Methods of Acquiring Citizenship in India

Every country has two types of people: citizens and aliens. Citizens are members of a country and owe loyalty to it. They enjoy political and civil rights. On the other hand, aliens are members of another country and do not enjoy all the rights as compared to the citizens.

In India, Article 5 to 11 of 'Part II' of the Constitution states certain rules about citizenship. However, it does not contain any provisions in detail. It seeks to identify people who became Indian citizens on the starting date of the constitution (26 January 1950).

Single Citizenship in India

The constitution of India talks about the federal structure and a dual polity (centre and states), but it only allows for single citizenship.

Indian citizens have their loyalty only to the union, and no provision has been established for separate state citizenship.

Other federal countries, such as the USA and Switzerland, have the provision for dual citizenship.

This means that in the USA, every person is treated as a citizen of the USA and also the state to which he/she belongs.

India brought in the concept of single citizenship from the British Constitution.

In India, because of single citizenship, all citizens enjoy equal civil and political rights all over the country, no matter in which state they belong.

Single citizenship promotes a feeling of unity and brotherhood among the citizens of the country.

Citizenship Act, 1955

The Citizenship Act, 1955 contains the provision for the acquisition and loss of citizenship after the inception of the Indian Constitution. This act has been revised several times over the years. It provides for citizenship by birth, descent, registration, naturalisation and incorporation of territory.

Citizenship of India by Birth

A person born on or after 26 January 1950 but before 1 July 1987 in India has been designated as an Indian citizen no matter the parents' nationality.

A person born on or after 1 July 1987 will be designated as a citizen only if either of their parents is an Indian citizen at the time of the person's birth.

For a person born after 3 December 2004, both or one of the parents should be Indian citizens during the time of his birth, and neither of them should be an illegal migrant in India.

The provision of citizenship by birth does not apply to the foreign diplomat posted in India.

Citizenship of India by Descent

A person who is born on or after 26th January 1950 but before 10th December 1992 and if his father was an Indian citizen during the time of his birth is considered an Indian citizen by descent.

For the person who is born out of India on or after 10th December 1992, the criteria for citizenship is that either of the parents should be an Indian citizen at the time of the person's birth.

The provision was altered after 3rd December 2004.

Now, a person who is born outside the territory of India will not be considered a citizen by descent, except if his birth is registered at an Indian Consulate within one year of birth.

After this time, the permission of the Central Government is required.

Citizenship of India by Registration

The Government of India may register a person as an Indian citizen if he is not an illegal migrant and meets the criteria presented below:

If he is of Indian origin and normally residing in India for seven years before applying.

If a person is married to an Indian citizen and is normally residing in India for seven years before the application.

If they are the children of persons who are Indian citizens.

If it is a person of full capacity and age, whose parents are successfully registered as Indian citizens.

An Indian origin person who is normally residing in any of the places or countries outside undivided India.

Citizenship of India by Naturalisation

The Indian Government grants a certificate of naturalisation on an application to a person who is not an illegal migrant and holds the qualifications given below:

If a person is not a citizen of any country where Indian citizens cannot apply for naturalisation.

If the application of a person for the process of naturalisation is accepted, then he has to renounce the citizenship of the present country.

He/she should be of good character.

The knowledge of a language mentioned in the Constitution's Eighth Schedule is required.

However, the government can waive off all the above-mentioned conditions for the person who has provided his service in the fields of science, literature, art, philosophy.

Citizenship of India by Incorporation of Territory

If a territory that belongs to a foreign country becomes part of India, then the Government of India specifies who the Indian citizen shall be among the people of that territory.

Citizens are the full members of a country who owe their loyalty to that country. In India, Article 5 to 11 of the Constitution identifies the citizens. Additionally, the Citizenship Act, of 1955 contains the provisions and conditions for citizenship. India has the provision of single citizenship, but various countries in the world have a system of dual citizenship.

Modes Of Losing Indian Citizenship

The Citizenship Act, 1955 also lays down the three modes by which an Indian citizen, whether a citizen at the commencement of the Constitution or subsequent to it, may lose his/her citizenship. It may happen in any of the three ways : renunciation, termination and deprivation.

Renunciation Of Citizenship [Section 8]

An Indian Citizen of full age and capacity can renounce his Indian citizenship by making a declaration to that effect and having it registered. But if such a declaration is made during any war in which India is engaged, the registration shall be withheld until the Central Government otherwise directs. When a male person renounces his citizenship, every minor child of him ceases to be an Indian citizen. Such a child may, however, resume Indian citizenship if he makes a declaration to that effect within a year of his attaining full age, i.e. 18 years.

Termination Of Citizenship [Section 9]

If a citizen of India voluntarily acquires the citizenship of another country, he shall cease to be a citizen of India. During the war period, this provision does not apply to a citizen of India, who acquires the citizenship of another country in which India may be engaged voluntarily. If any question arises as to whether, when or how any person has acquired the citizenship of another country, it is to be determined by such authority and in such manner as may be prescribed by the rules.

Deprivation Of Citizenship [Section 10]

Deprivation is a compulsory termination of citizenship of India. A citizen of India by naturalization, registration, domicile and residence, may be deprived of his citizenship by an order of the Central Government if it is satisfied that:

The citizen has obtained the citizenship by means of fraud, false representation or concealment of any material fact;

The citizen has shown disloyalty to the Constitution of India;

The citizen has unlawfully traded or communicated with the enemy during a war;

The citizen has, within five years after registration or neutralization, been imprisoned in any country for two years;

The citizen has been ordinarily resident out of India for seven years continuously.

Citizenship once acquired exists as a right of citizens, which cannot be otherwise taken away. Of course, ultimate powers rest with Parliament and it can terminate citizenship of any citizen through a law, but it has to be done through a valid Act of Parliament. Nothing less than that can affect the status of a person as a citizen. This has been provided under Article 10 of the Constitution of India.

Single Citizenship and Dual Citizenship

The constitution of India talks about the federal structure and a dual polity (centre and states), but it only allows for single citizenship.

Indian citizens have their loyalty only to the union, and no provision has been established for separate state citizenship.

Other federal countries, such as the USA and Switzerland, have the provision for dual citizenship.

This means that in the USA, every person is treated as a citizen of the USA and also the state to which he/she belongs.

India brought in the concept of single citizenship from the British Constitution.

In India, because of single citizenship, all citizens enjoy equal civil and political rights all over the country, no matter in which state they belong.

Single citizenship promotes a feeling of unity and brotherhood among the citizens of the country.

In India, only the Central Government is empowered to grant Citizenship to its Citizens.

On the other hand, in the other countries like US and Switzerland, both the Central Government and State Government are empowered to give Citizenship to its Citizens.

Natural Citizenship

Natural Citizenship is a kind of citizenship which can be acquired by birth.

A person born on or after 26 January 1950 but before 1 July 1987 in India has been designated as an Indian citizen no matter the parents' nationality.

A person born on or after 1 July 1987 will be designated as a citizen only if either of their parents is an Indian citizen at the time of the person's birth.

For a person born after 3 December 2004, both or one of the parents should be Indian citizens during the time of his birth, and neither of them should be an illegal migrant in India.

The provision of citizenship by birth does not apply to the foreign diplomat posted in India.

Citizenship by Naturalisation

The Indian Government grants a certificate of naturalisation on an application to a person who is not an illegal migrant and holds the qualifications given below:

If a person is not a citizen of any country where Indian citizens cannot apply for naturalisation.

If the application of a person for the process of naturalisation is accepted, then he has to renounce the citizenship of the present country.

He/she should be of good character.

The knowledge of a language mentioned in the Constitution's Eighth Schedule is required.

However, the government can waive off all the above-mentioned conditions for the person who has provided his service in the fields of science, literature, art, philosophy.

CHAPTER NINE

Civil Society and State

Introduction

Civil Society works for discharging several economic, social, cultural, moral and other responsibilities which fall in the domain of private activities. It, however, serves the public purpose of securing general welfare and development. The concept of Civil Society derives strength from the logic that a welfare state or a nation-state makes people dependent. It practises virtual authoritarianism in the name of welfarism. As such what is a need to a roll back of the state, the securing of a minimal state and a well developed active and determined civil society.

Initially, Civil Society used to be defined as a political community i.e. a society governed by the government, law and authority. In contemporary times, however, Civil Society is distinguished from the state and political community. It means non-governmental, private, voluntarily organized associations or institutions of the people, through which they try to secure their needs, desires and objectives. Such associations and organisations work independently of the government. Civil Society even opposes the wrong politics, decisions and projects of the government. In doing so, the civil society depends upon constitutional, peaceful and legal method of action.

In other words, Civil Society refers to the effective presence of autonomous groups and associations, business groups, interest groups, trade unions, voluntary social service organizations and clubs, in fact, all non-governmental organizations, clubs and groups working for securing their interests by their own efforts. It is important to identify the role of civil society in governance because there is actually a controversy about its role in relationship with the state. For example, Tocqueville (1969) argues that civil society is the most credible alternative to the state for the delivery of public goods. On the other hand, Hegel considers its role as being complimentary to that of the state and he puts a premium on the role of the state. Political Scientists such as Stephan (1998), Stocpol (1992) and Keane (1998) agree that civil society organisations are pre-requisite for making good governance. The World Bank and the United Nations also share the view that there can be no good governance without civil society.Civil society is pluralistic in meaning. Perhaps the most profound and enduring definition of the term is that of Locke (1963), who describes civil society as a contract between equals founded on the basis of voluntarism. Tocqueville builds on the definition provided by Locke and extends the concept further by introducing the idea of collective action as a way of curbing state tyranny for the purpose of producing the common good. Thus, the notion of civil society as a model of self-governance through voluntary effort for the delivery of common good was first introduced. Also, the ideas of voluntarism and collective action projected by these authors form the basis of democracy which is crucial for civil society.

Definitions

Early European political philosophers mainly defined civil society in the context of the relationship between the state and the society.

For Hobbes and even more clearly for Locke, the state originates in, is ultimately answerable to, and is therefore identified with (but not identical to) civil society.

For later philosophers, such as Montesquieu and Tocqueville, civil society stands at least partially in opposition to the state.

Marxists such as Gramsci identifies civil society with realms outside the power of the state. These definitions of civil society in relational terms are also reflected in recent literatures.

Fukuyama defined civil society as the realm of spontaneously created social structures separate from the state that underlie democratic political institutions.

To Dunn, civil society is broadly regarded as the domain of relationships which falls between the private realm of the family on the one hand and the state on the other.

Another way to define civil society is to restrict to the associational life of it.

Charles Taylor defined civil society as a web of autonomous associations independent of the state, which bind citizens together in matters of common concern and by their existence or actions could have an effect on public policy.

Schmitter defined civil society as a set or system of self-organized intermediary groups.

The Concise Oxford Dictionary of Politics defined civil society as the set of intermediate associations which are neither the state nor the (extended) family; civil society therefore includes voluntary associations and firms and other corporate bodies.

One of the advantages of this kind of definition is that civil society can thus be operationalized and be empirically tested on.

The latter kind of definitions is closely related with the former one.

As Tester sees it, civil society is the social relationships which involve the voluntary association and participation of individuals acting in their private capacities.

In a simple and simplistic formula, civil society can be said to equal the milieu of private contractual relationships.

We can regard the voluntary organizations as the institutionalization of the social relationships as defined by the former scholars.

Civil Society and Democracy

Friedman and Mckaiser argue that civil society and democracy are interdependent. According to them, democracy is the vehicle through which civil society can acquire a voice to speak for the people.

More recently, Edwards (2005) while exploring the ideas of some modern philosophers who project the idea of civil society as the public sphere (Habermas 1989) and the good society (Kant 1970), concludes that the idea of civil society remains compelling because it brings out the best in us and establishes lasting solutions for issues of inequalities, social injustice and poverty. Cohen and Arato (1992) distinguish civil society from the state and market and argue that it could become the needed instrument for expanding civil rights and democracy. This interpretation of the concept emphasises the idea of democracy which is also considered a necessary condition for good governance.

There are many other interpretations of this term by different theorists, but for the purpose of this discourse, civil society will encompass all collective actions by voluntary organisations within the public sphere for the purpose of delivering the common good. It will include activities of Non - Governmental Organizations (NGOs), Social Movements, informal and formal communal groups which collaborate with other institutional pillars to deliver goods of public value.

Civil societies play very important roles in democracy and governance. In the first instance, as advocates of the good society, they help to promote democratic principles and defend democratically elected governments. Secondly, they act as watchdogs to ensure prudent and efficient use of national resources. Lastly, they help to create public awareness on issues relating to good governance and develop a well- informed society. Dewey (1916) argues that the symbol of a good democracy is its ability to develop a well- informed society. Civil societies must be financially, politically and legally independent from government in order for them to effectively fulfil these roles. To succeed, they will also require the support of the political class, other arms of government and institutional pillars such as; anti -corruption bodies, directors of public prosecution, human rights bodies (TI Sourcebook, 2000).

South Africa – A Brief Description

South Africa as nation was for several years traumatized because of the struggle to overthrow the apartheid regime. However, in 1994, Nelson Mandela became the first president of post - apartheid South Africa, a National Unity Government was established comprising of the country's majority party; the African National Congress (ANC), the National Party and the Freedom Party. The government's major challenge was to rebuild the nation which had become politically, socially and economically devastated by so many years of conflict under the apartheid regime. The government immediately set up a Reconstruction and Development Programme (RDP), to address the issues of social inequalities, social injustice, infrastructural deficit, extreme poverty, massive unemployment deep seated insecurity and myriads of other socio- economic consequences of the years of the oppressive rule.

Under the RDP, the government designed a well - coordinated and sustainable programme to be executed with the cooperation of the different arms of government, together with civil society organisations and the private sector. The objective was to rebuild the nation within a peaceful and stable environment, characterised by sustainable development and economic growth. The political climate in South Africa changed significantly; the country attempted to embrace some of the neo- liberal economic policies of the West to come up with its own unique system which Andreason (2006) refers to as 'predatory liberalism'. In this model, the ruling African National Congress (ANC) adopted a strategy that enabled it to consolidate economic power in itself and effectively ward off opposition.

It is pertinent to state that there is a belief in some quarters that the anti – apartheid struggle was inspired by civil society organisations. This notion cannot be correct in view of the earlier claim that democracy and civil society are intimate bedfellows. The struggle that brought about the fall of apartheid in South Africa can best be described as resistance against racial oligarchy.

The Concept of Good Governance

Governance as a word connotes control, regulations and order. Court, Hyden and Mease describe governance as a system of regulations and rules within which social actors must take decisions for the purpose of creating social order. Swilling (1997) agrees that governance is the relationship between power structures to create "a civic public realm."

However, the idea that good governance is dependent on civil society makes the concept complex and pluralistic in meaning too. According to Warren (1999), liberal democrats will define a government as "good" only if it has the following attributes; freedom of information and freedom of the press, citizens capacity building strategy, upholds the fundamental human rights of citizens, encourages collective action and decision making, provides avenue for public opinion and institutional checks and balances.

Evans (2012) advances another idea of good governance premised on integrity in public administration. The Organisation for Economic Cooperation and Development (OECD), Transparency International (TI) and the United Nations Development Programme (UNDP) are some of the advocates of integrity as new public management strategy for the purpose of achieving accountable, transparent and responsible public institutions. In this model, the OECD identifies eight different criteria for good governance, which it calls "ethics infrastructure". They are "political commitment to integrity, effective legal frame work, efficient accountability mechanisms, workable codes of conduct, professional socialisation of staff, supportive public service conditions, an ethics coordinating body and an active society performing a watchdog role".

In this arrangement therefore, civil societies are assumed to be integrity agents and they are expected to monitor the activities of public institutions to ensure accountability, transparency, competence and responsiveness in public administration.

Grindle (2004), while criticizing modern day advocates of good governance agenda for not putting in place a priority list, advances the idea of 'good enough governance', which to him is more realistic. This model embodies important issues relating to culture, context and priority national developmental goals.

It is evident from the discourse above that good governance means different things in different context, but it has certain common attributes such as poverty reduction, accountability, transparency, minimum level of corruption, competent and efficient public service.

The Inter-face between Civil Society and Good Governance

It is also obvious from the discourse above, that the notions of civil society and good governance are closely linked. The two concepts share many distinct positive attributes necessary for achieving poverty reduction, sustainable development and economic stability and they are perceived as proffering solutions to most of the world's problems, irrespective of whether they are local, regional or global. However, Pelizzo contends that civil societies can become catalysts for the entrenchment of good governance only and when they make a demand on the political class to check and improve on the quality of governance. Uphoff also argues that civil socities are able to achieve greater level of development when they are independent from bureaucratic controls.

State

Society is a comprehensive term that includes all types of social organisations which men have formed to satisfy their needs and to achieve a full and happy life.

Society is nothing but a collection of individuals. It is within us and around us. Where ever life exists, there is society. Thus, a study of social organizations may not strictly fall within the scope of Political Science. It is also the job of civics and sociology which analyse the working of social organisations in detail. But as the students of Political Science, whose scope is confined to the study of the State, we should have knowledge of the State in detail.

The Meaning and Definition of State

Gettel has said, "Political Science is the science of state".

Gamer has observed, "Political Science begins and ends with the state."

State is the central focus of Political Science. It plays an important role in the society. It is the most powerful and universal social organisation. It is a rare and incomparable organisation.

It is a political organisation. There is no definite historical evidence about its creation. It seems that with the creation of society consisting of man was the need of state felt. State links individuals to groups and organisations, and establishes balance and reconciliation between individuals and groups. It provides security to individuals and safeguards their rights.

With the passage of time, the role of state has undergone change. It is one of the basic instincts of man to lead a disciplined life. In this respect the state is of help to the individual. The laws and rules of state help in establishing order and discipline in the society.

As man's nature forces him to live in a state, the state has been viewed as a natural institution. The state is regarded as a neutral, necessary and universal institution.

In common parlance, the word, 'state' is used in different ways. At times, it has been used as a synonym of 'nation', 'government', or society. The constituent units of a federation, in some cases, are also called states.

But in Political Science, 'state' has a specific meaning. To correctly understand the meaning of 'state', we may analyse different definitions of state.

In different times, the meaning and title of the word, 'state', have changed. In ancient times, Greeks used the word, 'state' in the sense of polis or city-state. Ancient Romans used the word civitas for 'state'.

The city-states in ancient Greece and Rome were small, simple and limited.

In the first part of the sixteenth century, Machiavellie, an eminent statesman of Italy, was the first to use the word La Stato. In his view, state is a 'power system'.

Towards the end of the sixteenth century, the French philosopher Bodin called state a 'republic'. He said that the state possessed sovereign power. In the seventeenth century, the British philosopher Hobbes argued that the state had unlimited power.

According to Aristotle, "The state is a union of families and villages and having for its ends a perfect and self-sufficing life by which we mean a happy and honourable life."

Jean Bodin said, "A state is an association of families and their possession governed by supreme power and by reason."

After this Thomas Hobbes, through his 'theory of complete sovereignty,' analysed the components of modern state.

Definitions of state have also been given by some eminent modern jurists and Political Scientists.

According to Bluntschli, "state is a politically organised people of a definite territory."

Woodrow Wilson defined state as "a people organised for law within a definite territory."

Burgess defined state as a "particular portion of mankind viewed as an organised unit."

Harold Laski defined state as "a territorial society divided into government and subjects claiming within its allotted physical area, a supremacy over all other institutions."

Oppenheim said, "The state exists when a people is settled in a country under its own sovereign government."

According to Gamer, "The state is a community of persons, more or less numerous, permanently occupying a definite portion of territory, independent (or nearly so) of external control and possessing an organised government to which the great body of inhabitants render habitual obedience."

There are different opinions as to the connotation of the term 'State'. It has been erroneously used as a synonym of 'country'; nation", 'society' and 'government'. In ordinary language, the word 'State' may mean many things. It may mean "condition". But in Political Science, the term 'State' has scientific and definite meaning.

In its scientific sense, it means a collection of human beings, occupying a definite territory under an organised government and subject to no outside control. It is the most universal and most powerful of all social institutions.

Where ever human beings live together for any length of time there exists some type of organization and authority and this constitutes the nucleus of the State.

Laski has rightly said that the study of politics "concerns itself with the life of men in relation to organised States". Hence, politics is nothing but a scientific study of the State.

There are different views regarding first emergence of the concept of the State. The Greeks used the word "Polis" which corresponds mostly to the English term "State". The

Greeks used the word "Polis" for "City-State".

The term was appropriate because at that time there were "City-States" in ancient Greece.

"Political Science" says Seeley "was for the Greeks largely municipal science."

The Romans used the term "Civitas" which also means the same thing. The Teutons employed the term "Status" which means existence.

The modern term "State" has been derived from the word "Status".

It was Niccolo Machiavelli (1969-1527) who first of all seems to have used the term "State" (the State) in Political Science. Thus, it becomes very clear that the term "State" was not very popular until the sixteenth century.

The concept of modern State was not known to the people living in a greater part of the Mediaeval Age. In the course of time, the concept became popular and "acquired the neutral sense of authority, pure and simple or constitution whatever its principles or direction."

Meaning of Sovereign State

A sovereign state is a political entity that is represented by one centralized government that has sovereignty over a geographic area. International law defines sovereign states as having a permanent population, defined territory, one government and the capacity to enter into relations with other sovereign states. It is also normally understood that a sovereign state is independent. According to the declarative theory of statehood, a sovereign state can exist without being recognised by other sovereign states. Unrecognised states will often find it difficult to exercise full treaty-making powers or engage in diplomatic relations with other sovereign states. All members of the UN are sovereign states, though not all sovereign states are necessarily members. Since the end of the 19th century, almost the entire globe has been divided into sections (countries) with more or less defined borders assigned to different states. Previously, quite large plots of land were either unclaimed or deserted, or inhabited nomadic peoples that were not organized into states. However, even in modern states, there are large remote areas that are not populated by people, such as the Amazon's tropical forests, they are uninhabited or inhabited exclusively or mainly by indigenous people (and some of them are still not in constant contact). There are also States that do not exercise de facto control over their entire territory, or where this control is disputed.

Currently, the international community includes more than 200 sovereign states, most of which are represented in the United Nations. These states exist in a system of international relations, where each state takes into account the policies of other states by making its own calculations. From this point of view, States are integrated into the international system of special internal and external security and legitimization of the dilemma. Recently, the concept of the international community has been formed to refer to a group of States that have established rules, procedures and institutions for the implementation of relations. Thus, the foundation for international law, diplomacy between officially recognized sovereign states, their organizations and formal regimes has been laid.

Westphalian sovereignty is the concept of nation-state sovereignty based on territoriality and the absence of a role for external agents in domestic structures. It is an international system of states, multinational corporations and organizations that began with the Peace of Westphalia in 1648.

Sovereignty is a term that is frequently misused. Up until the 19th century, the radicalised concept of a "standard of civilization" was routinely deployed to determine that certain people in the world were "uncivilized", and lacking organised societies. That position was reflected and constituted in the notion that their "sovereignty" was either completely lacking or at least of an inferior character when compared to that of the "civilized" people. Lassa Oppenheim said, "There exists perhaps no conception the meaning of which is more controversial than that of sovereignty. It is an indisputable fact that this conception, from the moment when it was introduced into political science until the present day, has never had a meaning, which was universally agreed upon." In the opinion of H.V. Evatt of the High Court of Australia, "sovereignty is neither a question of fact, nor a question of law, but a question that does not arise at all."

Sovereignty has taken on a different meaning with the development of the principle of self-determination and the prohibition against the threat or use of force as jus cogens norms of modern international law. The United Nations Charter, the Draft Declaration on Rights and Duties of States and the charters of regional international organizations express the view that all states are juridically equal and enjoy the same rights and duties based upon the mere fact of their existence as persons under international law. The right of nations to determine their own political status and exercise permanent sovereignty within the limits of their territorial jurisdictions is widely recognized.

In political science, sovereignty is usually defined as the most essential attribute of the state in the form of its complete self-sufficiency in the frames of a certain territory, that is its supremacy in the domestic policy and independence in the foreign one.

Named after the 1648 Treaty of Westphalia, the Westphalian System of state sovereignty, which according to Bryan Turner is "made a more or less clear separation between religion and state and recognized the right of princes 'to confessionalize' the state, that is, to determine the religious affiliation of their kingdoms on the pragmatic principle of cuiusregioeiusreligio [whose realm, his religion]."

Before 1900, sovereign states enjoyed absolute immunity from the judicial process, derived from the concepts of sovereignty and the Westphalian equality of states. First articulated by Jean Bodin, the powers of the state are considered to be suprema potestas within territorial boundaries. Based on this, the jurisprudence has developed along the lines of affording immunity from prosecution to foreign states in domestic courts. In The Schooner Exchange v. M'Faddon, Chief Justice John Marshall of the United States Supreme Court wrote that the "perfect equality and absolute independence of sovereigns" has created a class of cases where "every sovereign is understood to waive the exercise of a part of that complete exclusive territorial jurisdiction, which has been stated to be the attribute of every nation". Absolute sovereign immunity is no longer as widely accepted as it has been in the past and some countries including the United States, Canada, Singapore, Australia, Pakistan and South Africa have introduced restrictive immunity by statute, which explicitly limits jurisdictional immunity to public acts, but not private or commercial ones, though there is no precise definition by which public acts can easily be distinguished from private ones. State recognition signifies the decision of a sovereign state to treat another entity as also being a sovereign state. Recognition can be either expressed or implied and is usually retroactive in its effects. It does not necessarily signify a desire to establish or maintain diplomatic relations. No definition is binding on all the members of the community of nations on the criteria for statehood. In actual practice, the criteria are mainly political, not legal. L.C. Green cited the recognition of the unborn Polish and Czechoslovak states in World War I and explained that "since recognition of statehood is a matter of discretion, it is open to any existing State to accept as a state any entity it wishes, regardless of the existence of territory or of an established government." In international law, however, there are several theories of when a state should be recognised as sovereign. The constitutive theory of statehood defines a state as a person of international law if, and only if, it is recognised as sovereign by at least one other state. This theory of recognition was developed in the 19th century. Under it, a state was sovereign if another sovereign state recognised it as such. Because of this, new states could not immediately become part of the international community or be bound by international law and recognised nations did not have to respect international law in their dealings with them. In 1815, at the Congress of Vienna, the Final Act recognised only 39 sovereign states in the European diplomatic system, and as a result, it was firmly established that in the future new states would have to be recognised by other states and that meant in practice recognition by one or more of the great powers. One of the major criticisms of this law is the confusion caused when some states recognise a new entity, but other states do not. Hersch Lauterpacht, one of the theory's main proponents, suggested that a state must grant recognition as a possible solution. However, a state may use any criteria when judging if they should give recognition and they have no obligation to use such criteria. Many states may only recognise another state if it is to their advantage.

The State and Civil Society

Hegel's theory of the state, as was said above, depended upon the peculiar nature of the relationship existing, as he supposed, between the state and civil society. The relation is at once one of contrast and mutual dependence. The state as Hegel conceived it is no utilitarian institution, engaged in the commonplace business of providing public services, administering the law, performing police duties and adjusting industrial and economic interests.

All these functions belong to civil society. The state may indeed direct and regulate them as need arises, but it does not itself perform them. Civil society depends upon the state for intelligent supervision and moral significance. Considered by itself society would be governed only by the mechanical laws resulting from the interaction of the acquisitive and self-centered motives of many individuals.

The state, however, depends upon civil society for the means of accomplishing the moral purposes which it embodies. But though mutually dependent, the two stand on distinct dialectical levels. The state is not means but end. It represents the rational ideal in development and the truly spiritual element in civilization, and as such it uses, or perhaps in a metaphysical sense creates, civil society for the achievement of its own ends.

The state is the divine will, in the sense that it is mind present on earth, unfolding itself to be the actual shape and organization of a world.

Whereas civil society is a realm of blind inclination and causal necessity, the state acts in obedience to conscious ends, known principles and laws, which are not merely implied but expressly before its consciousness. Quotations of this sort might be multiplied indefinitely the state is the absolutely rational, the divinity which knows and wills itself, the eternal and necessary being of spirit, the march of God in the world.

It is important to observe, however, that the moral superiority thus attributed to the state implied no contempt for civil society or its institutions but in a sense the very opposite. Hegel, in his personal character and also in his political thought, was before everything else a good bourgeois, with rather more than the usual bourgeois respect for stability and security.

The relationship between the state and civil society, as he understood it, was mutual, even though it was also a relationship of superiority and inferiority and even though the authority of the state was absolute. The economic life of society gained moral significance-in a sense it was glorified-by the fact that the state and its cultural mission depend upon it.

But though the regulative power of the state is absolute, this does not extend to abolishing the institutions or the rights upon which the performance of economic functions depends. Property, according to Hegel's theory, is not created by the state or even by society but is an indispensable condition of human personality, much as it had been for Locke.

Hegel's account of civil society was in fact a careful, even an elaborate, analysis of the guilds and corporations, the estates and classes, the associations and local communities that made up the structure of the German society with which he was familiar. These or some equivalent he regarded as humanly indispensable. Without them the people would be merely formless mass and the individual would be merely a kind of human tom, since it is the context of economic and institutional ties that gives substance to his personality.

From Hegel's point of view, there are, the state is not composed primarily of individual citizens. The individual must be mediated through a long series of corporations and associations before he arrives at the final dignity of citizenship in the state.

Jacobinism, which makes government depend upon the will of the people expressed through the suffrage, means in practice government by a rabble. The people, meaning merely a section of citizens, is just that which does not know what it wills.

This view of civil society, it should be noted, had several aspects. On the one hand it might be regarded as reactionary. Undoubtedly it reflected the point of view of a society that was still securely stratified, that retained an unquestioning respect for rank and station, and that had never felt the levelling effects of industrialization.

It attached little or no value to equal citizenship which, in the light of French and English politics, appeared to be a condition of free government. Hegel's view of civil society, however, was not merely reactionary. It did not share the illusion of the utilitarian economists that part of the unchangeable order of nature but suggested rather Marx's treatment of it as a special phase of social development.

Hegel's point of view, moreover, was well adapted to a form of nationalism in which the state was assumed to have the function of fostering trade and industry as part of its general mission of extending national power. It must be admitted also that many of Hegel's criticisms of French Jacobinism were well taken.

In the name of liberty it often destroyed quite recklessly forms of social organization that served a useful purpose and that in one form or another had to be reinstated in the interest of liberalism itself. In general Hegel's view of civil society embodied a sound principle that when the individual is regarded merely as a citizen, the state tends to absorb all forms of human association.

And in effect this is not liberty but despotism, as all forms of political totalitarianism prove. The arguments of the political Pluralists at the end of the nineteenth century could very largely have been constructed out of Hegel's theory of civil society. The importance that Marx attached to economic forces in politics quite definitely hag its roots here, even though Marx doomed Hegel's state to extinction.

The theory of civil society and its relation to the state largely determined the meaning that Hegel attached to constitutional government. The state's power as he conceived it is absolute but it is not arbitrary. Its absolutism reflected its superior moral position and the fact that Hegel permitted the state to monopolize the ethical aspects of society.

The state, however, must always exercise its regulative powers under the forms of law. It is an embodiment of reason and law is rational. This meant for Hegel that the acts of a public authority must be predictable because they proceed from known rules, that the rules limit the discretionary powers of officials, and that official action expresses the authority of the office and not the private will or judgment of the office-holder.

The law must bear equally on all the persons to whom it applies because, being general, it cannot consider individual peculiarities. The essence of despotism is lawlessness, and the essence of a free and constitutional government is that it excludes lawlessness and produces security.

Despotism means any state of affairs where law has disappeared and where the particular will as such, whether of a monarch or a mob, counts as law or rather takes the place of law.

It is precisely the fact that everything in the state is fixed and secure which is the bulwark against caprice and dogmatic opinion.

Hegel's state, therefore, was what later German jurisprudence came to call a Rechtsstaat. It had to achieve a high order of internal administrative efficiency and its judicial system in particular had to give security to rights of property and of the person, which Hegel regarded as indispensable to the economic functions of civil society. His theory of constitutional government was therefore in accord with that of liberalism in distinguishing between legal authority and personal power, but it acknowledged no relationship between the rule of law and democratic political processes.

The key to this phase of Hegel's constitutionalism was the high importance that he attached to an official governing class, the universal class as he called it, which by birth and training is fitted to rule and which embodies a long tradition of hierarchical authority and orderly procedure.

Such a class he regarded as detached from and impartial toward the private and social interests which it regulates. In a special sense, therefore, it represents the general will and the reason of society, in contrast with acquisitive self-interest or special and partial interests, and is the guardian of the whole public interest.

The bureaucratic organization of civil society is its apex, the point at which it makes contact, so to speak, with the still higher institutions of the state. The essential property of the whole system is that it is rooted in immemorial custom, in long accepted grades of rank and authority, and yet that these grades are functions in the total life of the nation.

This conception of constitutional government was contrasted in Hegel's mind with French experiments in the making of paper constitutions and also with English parliamentary government. For the former he had an historian's deep-seated contempt. To ask who makes a constitution, he said, is nonsense, for constitutions are not made.

A constitution is not just something manufactured it is the work of centuries. It must be treated as something simply existent in and by itself, as divine therefore, and constant. Bills of rights, the separation of powers, checks and balances, therefore, are mere apparatus. Constitutionalism depends on a tradition of self-government, and in Hegel's opinion this tradition is inseparable from differences of social rank, an acceptable balance between a governing class and the lower orders of society, and an aristocracy characterized by its loyalty to the crown.

The principal function of the monarchy is to maintain this balance. But the balance depends not on a separation of powers but on a distinction of functions, and the purpose of the distinction is not to weaken but to strengthen the state.

The English parliamentary system, on the other hand, appeared to Hegel to be a degenerate remnant of feudalism. In it political power had remained the private perquisite of an aristocratic oligarchy which had no national function. Hence England had never achieved the dignity of a state.

Perhaps in the year of Hegel's death this was a not unrealistic, if somewhat shortsighted, estimate of English government. Hegel's earliest political conviction was a thoroughgoing dislike of government by a vested aristocratic interest as he saw it exhibited in the city of Bern.

His maturest judgment, set down almost at the time of his death, was that English government belonged to that type. It lacked, he said, der grosse Sinn von Fursten, and he predicted that the Reform Bill would merely add the fallacies of Jacobinism to those of feudalism. According to Hegel's reading of constitutional history the significant step was the rise of national authority under the monarchy, not the control of the executive by the legislature.

In comparison with the part assigned to officialdom, both representative institutions and the monarchy played a minor role in Hegel's theory of constitutionalism, in spite of the mystical reverence that he gave to the monarchy. For reasons already made clear Hegel regarded representation on the basis merely of territory and population as meaningless, since the individual in his relation to the state figures as a member of one or more of the many associations supported by civil society.

The legislature is the point at which these associations meet the state. What needs to be represented, on the side of civil society, are the significant spheres (Kreise) or interests or functional units. The difficulties that this idea of functional representation have encountered in the lust quarter century make clear the reason why Hegel never arrived at any practicable plan of representative government on that principle.

On the other hand, he considered it essential that the official class, which must regulate civil society, should be represented in the legislature by the ministers. But the latter are in no sense responsible to the legislature. On the contrary the legislature, as Hegel conceived it, stands in substantially an advisory or consultative relation to the ministry, which is responsible to the crown.

The monarch, however, according to Hegel, has no considerable power and such power as he has ought, in a well regulated monarchy, to flow from his legal position as head of the state.

In a well-organized monarchy, the objective aspect belongs to law alone; the monarch's part is merely to set to the law the subjective, I will.

The monarch is in fact a kind of visible symbol for abstractions like national spirit, national law and national state which Hegel conceived to be the real forces in the background of politics and history.

CHAPTER TEN

Is Democracy Compatible with Economic Growth?

Introduction

The debate on the question of Democracy and economic growth became an issue of political discussion in the context of under developed countries of Asia, Africa and Latin America. Most of these countries achieved independence from the colonial rulers during the decade of 1940's and 1950's. After the independence, most of these countries proclaimed some sort of democratic system as the ultimate goal. However, soon a majority of them turned in to authoritarian rule, open dictatorships or military junta whether it was Pakistan, Myanmar, Indonesia, Taiwan, Singapore, Nigeria, Cuba etc. The exigencies of growth and survival compelled them to all political opposition and denial of civil and political liberties to their citizens. This raised the fundamental question—what come first : democracy or growth? In other words what should be given preference-giving civil political liberty and rights, democratic freedom and get the consent of its citizens for government policies or removing poverty, illiteracy and misery of the people through an authoritarian regime. One school of thought preferred to go ahead with the ideals of democracy and the promotion of civil rights whereas the other school of thought preferred to remove poverty, hunger and unemployment and provide economic growth with the help of authoritarian regimes before providing civil rights to the citizens of their country.

Meaning of Economic Growth

Economic growth means an increase in a country's national output which can be caused by the maximization in the value of goods and services produced by agrarian, industrial and all other sector of the economy. It can be measured by the increase or decrease in a country's gross domestic product (GDP). Of more importance in the growth of the ratio of GDP to population, this is also called per capita income. The growth may be increased caused by more efficient use of inputs is referred to intensive growth. However, GDP growth caused only by increase in inputs such as capital, population or territory is called extensive growth. Economic growth is generally differentiated from development economics. The economic growth is primarily the study of how countries can advance their economies. On the other hand the development economics is the study of the economic aspects of the development process in low-income countries. Nobel prize winner in economics (1971) Professor Simon Kuzents think that the "economic growth is a long term rise in capacity to supply increasingly by diverse economic goods to its population, the growing capacity based on advancing technology and the institutional and ideological adjustment that is demands". Professor Kuzents has mentioned six characteristics features manifested in the growth process : (a) High rates of growth per capita output and population (b) High rates of increase in total factor productivity, especially labour productivity (c) High rates of structural transformation of the economy (d) High rates of social and ideological transformation (e) The prosperity of economically developed countries to reach out to the rest of the world for markets and raw materials (f) Limited spread of development to only a third of the world population. Economic growth results in the increase of general welfare of the community. It means rise in the private consumption of goods and services and expansions of social services like public health and public instruction. It also means rise in the living standard of the citizens. It would also be necessary to not that the fast economic growth may involve depletion of non-renewable natural resources and environmental pollution. Then government can take special measure to secure faster rate of economic growth. For example, it can reduces taxes to induce people to spend more money. It can increase money supply and reduce interest rates to raise the level of expenditure of the people. Moreover, the government can give some concession to encourage people to set up new industries.

Relationship Between Democracy and Economic Growth

Generally, Democracy as a term is used to denote 'liberal democracy' which implies certain institutions and procedures. It is a form of government based on people's mandate and balance the principle of limited government against the ideal of popular consent. Its liberal characters are reflected in a network of internal and external checks upon government that are designed to guarantee liberty and afford citizens protection against the state. Its democratic features are based upon a system of regular and competitive elections, conducted on the basis of universal adult suffrage and political equality. According to Andrew Haywood the core features of liberal democratic regime are: (a) constitutional government based upon formal, usually legal rules; (b) guarantee of civil liberties and individual rights by the constitution; (c) institutional fragmentation and a system of checks and balances; (d) regular elections respecting the principles of universal adult suffrage and one person, one vote; (e) political pluralism in the form of electoral choice and a party competition; (f) a healthy civil society in which organized groups and interests enjoy independence from government; (g) a capitalist or private enterprise economy organised along market lines.

The economic freedom in the liberal democracies promotes economic growth or the per capita income. In 1959, Lipset gave a theory that more well to do nation, the best are its chances to maintain democracy. As a country develops economically, its society and people develop the skills needed to sustain democracy faster and better.

Adam Przeworski and Limongi after studying the period 1950-1991 had calculated that in a democratic county that has a per capita income of under $ 1500, the regime has a life of eight years, with $ 1500-3000, it is 18 years and above $ 6000, it is stable. About two-thirds of democratic countries which had the per capita income of $ 9000 have been the most stable. The views on the relationship between democracy and economic growth have changed by the time to time. As Rodrik in his recent empirical studies based on samples of more than 100 countries suggests that there is small reason to believe that democracy is conducive to lower growth over long time spans. Similarly, Barro's model of economic growth covers three time decade periods (1965-75, 1975-85, 1985-90). He explain the following measures of correlation between democracy and economic growth: (a) It controls included in it are: initial income, initial level of human capital (health, schooling), educational spending, fertility rate, government consumption, market distortions (black market premium, rule of law), investment terms and trade, (b) among democracy variable like political rights and civil liberties are included, (c) Although not so significant, but positive effect is seen if some of the controls are not included while measuring the correlation between the two, (d) However, relationship between democracy and economic growth is nonlinear. At the low levels of democracy, more political rights foster growth but is reaches a peak at middle levels. Let us now discuss the arguments for and against democracy versus economic growth.

Democracy and Economic Growth are not compatible

The arguments by various scholars has been developed, in the context of economic growth for the developing nations that democratic freedoms and rights are almost a basic human rights and economic development does not mean more economic growth measured in terms of GDP growth and in the profits of large companies and businesses, but a more holistic phenomenon where how exactly the wealth is distributed, how many children are going to school and whether there are provisions for health care for everybody are more important. This view sees a connection between political freedoms and the fulfilment of economic needs. They also argue that political freedom can have a major role in providing relevant information in solving and fulfilling the economic needs and in providing incentives. There have been many noteworthy examples of rapid growth in some countries under liberal authoritarian regimes that has lent credence to the view that democracy is an impediment to growth. For instance Taiwan, South Korea, Singapore, China, Indonesia have had authoritarian governments that were able to take fast decisions and implement them that has lead to rapid growth in these countries.

The liberal capitalist school of thought who insists on seeing democracy is an impediment to growth advance three basic arguments. First, that democratic rights and freedoms hamper economic growth and development. This view is called as the 'Lee Thesis' after former Singapore Prime Minister Lee Kuan Yew who was an ardent proponent of it. Second, if people are given a choice between political freedom and fulfilling economic needs, people will invariably choose growth to rid themselves of economic misery and deprivation. They would not care for democracy. Third, liberal political freedoms are a western cultural priority and obsession and culturally it is not that important for some cultures like those to be formed in the middle-east and Asia. In Asian cultures, order and discipline which facilitates prosperity are more important. As Lee Kuan Yew commented, "I do not believe that democracy necessarily leads to development. I believe that what a country needs to develop is discipline more than democracy". The so called Asian Tiger economies have all followed system that has been from less than democratic to quite dictatorial. This school of thought argues what is the need for democratic rights and duties when governments think about and work for the welfare of its citizens. They have argued since collective goals are clear, principally of economic growth, the government job of delivering on them should not be hampered by democratic checks and balances. Przeworski and Limongi views — the favourable effects between democracy and economic development as single directional, that is, economic development leads to democracy, but democracy retards economic development. Therefore democracy would be directly related with economic level, but inversely related with economic growth. They further says that — Since wealthy countries might have reached high economic level for other reasons, but would slow down after democracy is established, while for poor countries economic development has not create a favourable environment for democracy, but thus they would also enjoy economic growth not retarded by democracy. Almost all the advanced economics of the world, including the United States, Japan, Germany, Grait Britain, Russia, etc. and also almost all the emerging economies in contemporary world, made their initial take-off and fastest growth under non-democracy we have in mind today. This view can be stretched as for as stating that, dictatorships are needed to generate development. Norwegian social scientist Jon Elster views that — democracy does not necessarily lead to economic development, nor the other way round, even though democracy is not necessarily the best form of government for poor countries from the perspective of economic development. The point is economic development can not and should not justify simply because it is not yet clear whether democracy is more effective than its alternatives in bringing about economic development. The economic considerations can be nothing more than just an instrumental point of view and if we regard it is a sufficient justification for non-democratic regimes. Economic growth does not bother democratic value. The main purpose of economic growth is to promote economic rights only. The ideology of growth constitutes indeed, the dominant social paradigm, in both West and the East. According to Serge Latouche, "Although the growth economy is the offspring of the dynamic of the market economy, the two concepts should not be confused since it is possible to have a growth economy which is not also a market economy-notably the case of actually existing socialism". Growth economy can be defined as the system of economic organisation that is geared either "objectively" or deliberately, towards maximising economic growth. The growth economy have been already created a growth society, the main features of this society are consumerism, privacy, alienation and the subsequent disintegration of social ties.

Democracy and Economic Growth are Compatible

Noble Laureate economist Amartya Sen in his book Development as Freedom has argued that democracy and economic growth are not linked and need not to be incompatible. He pointed out for instance that country like Botswana which was a democracy but yet achieved a fast rate of growth. He argued that countries that had developed under authoritarian systems developed not because of the dictatorial styles but because of other policies like high levels of literacy, presence of basic facilities like health care, land reforms, use of international markets, open competition etc. Amartya Sen also argued that growth should not mean increase in GDP but also in the quality of lives capabilities of the citizens. He makes the point that civil and political rights give the people an opportunity to draw attention to their exact demands and guide policy making and implementation towards those policies. The democratic government respond to pressure and for that pressure by the electorate there is need for a highly developed environment of rights and freedoms. He also contested the view that poor people will necessarily choose economic rewards and need fulfilment over political rights. He further argued that people do need and demand dignity and basic human rights and its wrong to argue that people will be willing to barter that away.

Sen classified the importance of democratic system in economic growth and development into three categories : (i) democracy has an intrinsic value, (ii) and an instrumental value and (iii) and plays an important role in the creation of value and norms.

Sen explains human beings naturally value unrestrained participation in social and political activities. The absence of democratic rights and freedoms may be fine when everything is going fine and there is economic prosperity but when situations crumble and there is need for protest and to make opinions known, the lack of a culture and environment of democratic protest and dissent is badly missed in authoritarian regimes. According to Amartya Sen, democracy has an intrinsic value to growth. As the political incentives provided by democratic governance acquire practical value at these times. The culture of political freedoms and civil rights also plays a major part in helping the formation of value and in the identification of needs. About the instrumental value, Sen argues the ultimate objective of economic growth is the realisation of human freedom. And to that extant democracy has an instrumental value. The instrumental role of freedom has many components like economic facilities, political freedoms, social opportunities, transparency, guarantees and protective security. He point out that economic needs and political freedoms are linked constructively. The exercise of political rights lead to a policy response from the government to economic needs and the formulation and conceptualisation of economic needs need the presence of political rights. Democracy provides an opportunity to work its processes and institutions and use it for growth and development. So ultimately the success of democracy will depend on the use that people put to it. A democratic set up thus can be very valuable and people society have always be on the lookout to make it even more successful this development, growth and social justice depends on the quality of functioning and practices of democratic institutions. Another view has given by economists Edwards Glaeser — that it is economic growth which stimulates democracy or the adoption of better institutions and not the opposite. They further make the point that — the accumulation of human capital is a more important determinant of economic growth than political institutions. They study a group of countries in the period of 1960 to 2000 and classifying them into four categories (a) Autocracies (b) imperfect autocracies (c) imperfect democracies and (d) stable (or perfect) democracies. Their analysis of democracy captures basic government practices in a combination of institutional and behavioural indicators such as competitiveness of executive recruitment, competitiveness of political participation, openness and constraints on the executive.

They found that in 2000 nearly all countries with high levels of education were classified as stable democracies and nearly all stable democracies were highly educated. In contrast, the economists believe that nearly all countries run by dictators were poorly educated. Glaeaser also find that as much as education levels increased, democracies were more common, albeit many imperfect. Political Scientist Mathew Baum and David Lake have noticed significant indirect effects of democracy on growth through its effects on education and public health. Both education and health have large social advantages even when they are privately provided, therefore, investment in these sectors is subject to be influenced by public policy. Baum and Lake noticed that development of democracy in poor countries improves the life expectancy of women, whereas increasing democracies in more developed countries improves secondary education enrolment of women. They also describe that both life expectancy and secondary education have positive impacts on GDP per capita growth.

Milton Friedman in his book Capitalism and Freedom (1962) believes that, more democratic political rights will reinforce economic rights and therefore will be beneficial to economic development. On the other hand, the assurance of the individual's economic freedom result in and is predicted upon the maintenance of a free-enterprise exchange economy that constitutes an ideal economic arrangement for a free society. He also stressed that — some activities of the democratic government, such as income redistribution, would tend to retard economic development, these activities are not peculiar to democracies. According to Walter Galenson and Karl de Schweinitz, that democracy of poor nations unwilling pressures for immediate consumption, which resulted at the cost of investment, hence of growth. Galenson describe that the role of trade union and the governments is most important in terms of growth. He noticed that the more democratic a government is, the greater the diversion of resources from investment to consumption. Schweinitz analyzed that, if trade unions and labour parties are successful in securing a larger share of the national income and limiting the freedom for action of entrepreneurs, they may have the effect of restricting investment surplus so much that the rate of economic growth is inhibited. Democracy was thus seen as inimical to economic development. Przeworski discuss that poor people have a higher propensity to consume. That is why democracy may be compatible with economic growth at high but not at low levels of income. The under mention model of growth attributes it to the increase of the stock of physical capital. And democracy is always responsive to the pressure for immediate consumption.

The chain of reasoning to thus the following:

(a) poor people want to consume immediately,

(b) when markets can organize, they drive wages up, reduce profits and reduce investment,

(c) when people can vote, government distributes income away from investment,

(d) lowering investment slow down the growth.

Thus, democracy allocates better the available resources to productive uses and better protection of property rights, thus allowing a longer term perspective to investors. There is also a definite sense that by allowing freely flow of information, democracies improve the quality of economic decisions.

Samuel Phillips Huntington relates economic development with political stability or a democratic stability. He pointed — that what matters for economic development is political stability, rather than the particular political institutions. Political instability effects economic performance only under dictatorship whether because of institutional constraints or of motivations of those who govern democracies, neither past nor expected changes of heads of governments affects growth under democracies. But under the dictatorships, economic growth slow down significantly when the tenure of rulers is threatened. The same is true of various forms of socio-political unrest like strikes, anti-government demonstration and riots occur more often in democracies but they retard growth only in dictatorship.

According to Andrew Richard, the evidence clarifying that democracy is fully compatible with the market and through that with the economic efficiency is overwhelming. Yet new democratic nations have generally been established in hard times. And the international situations in which these new democracies have operated has been globalised. Yet, evidence showing that those nations having the democratic system are more stable and establishing the higher levels of development and economic growth. It is also finds that an equal distribution of income leads to democratic stability. Therefore social and conditions have considerable effects on new democratic regimes that whether thay can last and function effectively.

Conclusion

From the above discussion, I would conclude that democracy with economic growth are compatible, but to remove various challenges in this competitive world. The various evidence suggesting that democracy should not be sacrificed on the alter of development. For the last fifty years the various countries that developed under the democratic government, having faster growth of per-capita income, because of lower rates of population growth, economic and political freedoms, social justice and equality. So, democracy is essential not because it can bring about every kinds of economic development, but also to given the opportunities to better living conditions for their citizens. As Amartya Sen argued that — democracy has constructive importance, in addition to its intrinsic value for the lives of the citizens and its instrumental importance in political decisions. The claims of democracy as a universal value have to take not of this diversity of considerations. On the other hand, various developing countries choose the option to remove poverty, hunger and shelter and provide economic growth with the help of the authoritative regimes over democracies. The countries like Taiwan, South Korea, Singapore, Hong Kong, having higher rates of growth without adopting a democratic system. As the former prime minister of Singapore argued that authoritarian governance is the better in the interest of economic growth, as the Asian values are not much supportive freedom and more linked with order and discipline and claiming of human rights in the areas of civil and political liberties, therefore, these values are not relevant and less appropriate in Asian region than in the west. But the question still remains that, growth without giving civil and political liberties, social justice, would be perfect. As the evidence shows that women are particularly affected by the authoritarian regimes. Their participation in gainful activities is not significant at the same rates as far as democracy is concerned. On the other hand Authoritarians regime uses coercive power to prevent people from expressing their dissent and to repress workers. Because Authoritarians believes in rule by force, they are highly vulnerable to any visible signs to dissent. They may be successful economically only if they are stable, if no one think that dictator would change or the dictatorial would be abolished. Thus, both democracy and non-democracies have their limitations regarding the achievement of economic goals. Inspite of many flows, democracy is the better option, but it needs to be strengthened and secured.

CHAPTER ELEVEN

ON WHAT GROUND IS CENSORSHIP JUSTIFIED AND WHAT ARE ITS LIMITS?

Censorship is a means whereby the information people receive is limited, either wholly or in part by another individual or a group or individuals. Censorship has occurred in varying forms for centuries and happens within all aspects of society. Parents and teachers censor what children see and read, the government censor the information available to the public and everybody, whether realise it or not partake in self-censorship. It is argued that there are many reasons for censorship, but the two that are most agreed upon are firstly to protect vulnerable adults and children, this occurs mostly within the media and entertainment industry by making sure films and games have age restrictions and secondly to control people's behaviours and to sway their thoughts towards one indirectly dictated opinion. This is the motive that is felt is behind the majority of the government's actions and equally some actions within religion. If people have limited information, than the freedom to formulate and individual opinion is withheld. Most people feel that censorship is immoral and the public have a right to the truth and should be allowed to formulate and fully informed opinion regardless of consequences. Censorship in the case of what children witness is widely disputed. Most believe that it is a necessity to protect children from violent games as they believe it affects children's perception of acceptable behaviour and disrupts children's development.

The term censorship refers to the suppression, banning or deletion of speech, writing or images that are considered to be indecent, obscene or otherwise objectionable. Censorship becomes a civil rights issue when a government or other entity with authority, suppresses ideas or the expression of ideas, information and self. In the U.S., censorship has been debated for decades as some seek to protect the public from offensive materials and others seek to protect the public's rights to free speech and expression.

What is Censorship

The word censorship is derived from the Latin word censere, which is "to give as one's opinion, to assess." In Roman times, censors were public officials who took census counts as well as evaluating public principles and moralities. Societies throughout history have taken on the belief that the government is responsible for shaping the characters of individuals, many engaging in censorship to that end.

In his text The Republic, ancient Greek philosopher Plato makes a systematic case for the need for censorship in the arts. Information in the ancient Chinese society was tightly controlled, a practice that persists in some form today. Finally, many churches, including the Roman Catholic Church, have historically banned literature felt to be contrary to the teachings of the church.

Censorship in America

Many of America's laws have their origins in English law. In the 1700s, both countries made it their business to censor speech and writings concerning sedition, which are actions promoting the overthrowing of the government and blasphemy, which is sacrilege or irreverence toward God. The idea that obscenity should be censored didn't gain serious favor until the mid-1800s. The courts in both countries, throughout history, have worked to suppress speech, writings and images on these issues.

As time went on, contention arose over just what should be considered "obscene." Early English law defined obscenity as anything that tended to "deprave and corrupt those whose minds are open to such immoral influences," and anything that "might suggest to the minds of the young of either sex and even to persons of more advanced years, thoughts of a most impure and libidinous character." This essentially meant anything that might lead one to have "impure" thoughts. This definition carried over into early American law as well.

Censorship in America took a turn in 1957, when the U.S. Supreme Court declared that adults cannot be reduced to reading "only what is fit for children," ruling that it must be considered whether the work was originally meant for children or adults. Still, the Court acknowledged that works that are "utterly without redeeming social importance" can be censored or banned. This left another vague standard for the courts to deal with.

Censorship in America is most commonly a question in the entertainment industry, which is widely influential on the young and old alike. Public entertainment in the form of movies, television, music and electronic gaming are considered to have a substantial effect on public interest. Because of this, it is subject to certain governmental regulations.

Censorship and the First Amendment

The First Amendment to the U.S. Constitution prohibits suppression of an individual's right to free speech, stating "Congress shall make no law ... abridging the freedom of speech, or of the press ..." This is a principle held dear by those protesting censorship in any form. In the U.S., censorship of obscene materials in entertainment is allowed in order to protect children from pornography and other offensive things. The problem with government sanctioned censorship is the risk of violating the civil rights of either those producing the materials, or those wishing to view them.

Censorship Example in the Film Industry

The issue of censorship in the film industry has, at times, been quite contentious. In an effort to avoid the censorship issue, while striving to protect children and conform to federal laws, the Motion Picture Association of America ("MPAA") instituted a self-regulating, voluntary rating system in 1968. In the 1990s, the MPAA updated its rating system, making it easier for parents to determine what is appropriate for their children, based on the children's ages.

The MPAA rating system has a number of ratings. Rather than censoring movies or their content by exclusion of content, MCAA ratings are assigned by a board of people who view the movies, who consider such factors as violence, sex, drug use and language when assigning ratings. The board strives to assign a rating that a majority of parents in the U.S. would give, considering their needs to protect their children.

Landmark Ruling on Censorship of Magazine Sales

In the mid-1960s, Sam Ginsberg, who owned Sam's Stationery and Luncheonette on Long Island was charged with selling "girlie" magazines to a 16-year old boy, which was in violation of New York state law. Ginsberg was tried in the Nassau County District Court without a jury and found guilty. The judge found that the magazines contained pictures which, by failing to cover the female buttocks and breasts with an opaque covering were harmful to minors. He stated that the photos appealed to the "prurient, shameful or morbid interest of minors," and that the images were patently offensive to standards held by the adult community regarding what was suitable for minors.

Ginsberg was denied the right to appeal his convictions to the New York Court of Appeals, at which time he took his case to the U.S. Supreme Court, on the basis that the state of New York had no authority to define two separate classes of people (minors and adults), with respect to what is harmful. In addition, Ginsberg argued that it was easy to mistake a young person's age and the law makes no requirement for how much effort a shop owner must put into determining age before selling magazines intended for adult viewing. The Court did not agree, holding that Ginsberg might be acquitted on the grounds of an "honest mistake," only if he had made "a reasonable bonafide attempt to ascertain the true age of such a minor." The conviction was upheld.

Contemporary Political Issues and Censorship

Internet Censorship refers to the suppression of information that can be published to or viewed on the internet. While many people enjoy unfettered access to the broad spectrum of information racing across the information highway, others are denied access or allowed access only to government approved information. Rationales for internet censorship range from a desire to protect children from content that is offensive or inappropriate to a government's objective to control its people's access to world news, opinions and other information.

In the United States, the First Amendment affords the people some protection of their right to freely access the internet and of the things they post to the web. Because of this, there is very little government-mandated "filtering" of information that originates in the U.S. The issue of censorship of certain content, especially content that may further terrorism is constantly debated at the federal government level.

As an example of censorship, the following countries are known for censoring their people's internet content:

North Korea – only about 4% of the people have access to the internet and the only content allowed is government-controlled.

Burma – the government filters the people's emails and blocks access to any sites or information exposing human rights violations in the country.

Saudi Arabia – the government blocks nearly half a million websites, especially those that discuss religious, social or political topics that conflict with the beliefs of the monarchy.

Iran – the government censors information coming into and going out of the nation. Bloggers are required to register with the Ministry of Art and Culture. Any who express opinions contrary to those of the governmental leaders are harassed and put in jail.

China – the government enforces the harshest program of internet censorship in the world. While users have access to some form of internet, their searches are filtered, sites are blocked and searches on such issues as Taiwan independence, the Tiananmen Square Massacre or other controversial issues to sites that offer information that is more flattering to the Communist Party.

In other words, Internet censorship is control or suppression of the publishing or accessing of information on the Internet. The legal issues are similar to offline censorship.

One difference is that national borders are more permeable online, residents of a country that bans certain information can find it on websites hosted outside the country. A government can try to prevent its citizens from viewing these even if it has no control over the websites themselves.

Filtering can be based on a blacklist or be dynamic. In the case of a blacklist, that list is usually not published. The list may be produced manually or automatically.

Barring total control on Internet connected computers, such as in North Korea, total censorship of information on the Internet is very difficult (or impossible) to achieve due to the underlying distributed technology of the Internet. Pseudonymity and data havens (such as Freenet) allow unconditional free speech, as the technology guarantees that material cannot be removed and the author of any information is impossible to link to a physical identity or organization.

Developing Countries and the Question of Censorship

Social networks have become powerful tools in the lives of many people in third world countries. Social media sites are where people go to acquire knowledge and ideas from other individuals. People use them as platforms through which they communicate with their relatives and friends.

Social media sites are relatively cheap means of communication in third world countries. However, the question has been the extents to which one can exercise freedom via the sites. Freedom of social media sites is only possible in democratic countries.

Censorship of social media sites is the control of information that is available to users. In many cases, governments control the activities of social media sites. However, other people and institutions can also censor social media sites.

Social networks make it easy for people to obtain and distribute information rapidly. However, dictatorial regimes cannot tolerate the idea of free flow of information. Many dictatorial regimes are in third world countries. Such regimes have noted the impacts that social media sites have on human societies.

In Tunisia, the actions of a fruit vendor sparked protests in the entire country. The death of the vendor sparked protests in Tunisia, Libya, Egypt, Syria and Iran. The protests spread to other countries through information passed via social media sites.

Last year, Britain experienced civil unrest and protests. People posted images of riots in social network sites. Plans used in the execution of the riots were also passed through the sites. This made some politicians call for the shutdown of social media to limit the flow of information and awareness.

The communist party that rules China also views freedom of the sites as a threat to the authority. These show that developed countries also feel that social media sites should be censored.

Arguments that oppose censorship of the social media are based on the belief that the sites are a platform through which individuals exercise their rights. Opponents of censorship argue that every person has a right to express himself freely.

People should express their ideas, receive and disseminate information freely. Moreover, social media is currently used in execution of business deals that are beneficial. Nonetheless, education on utilization of the sites is essential. Users must be educated on how to use the sites to avoid conflict with the dictatorial regimes.

Proponents of censorship of social network sites normally argue that it is necessary for maintenance of peace within a country. They have noted the impacts that the sites have on human actions.

Some regimes feel that social sites can be used to leak information that can lead to the imposition of sanctions. Usually, they provide political reasons for censorship of the sites. They propose that censorship is necessary to control activities of people who oppose the regime in power.

Other reasons for censorship are based on religious and social life issues. Governments may censor the sites to control religious activities of the citizens.

This is common in third world countries in Asia where Islam is practiced. For example, approximately 400,000 websites were censored in Saudi Arabia to control religious and women's activities.

Hence, in third world countries, censorship is implemented to control activities of political and religious organizations. It is also implemented to suppress activities of minority and terrorist groups. Governments use various methods to censor the sites.

One method is the employment of spies who monitor posts that citizens make. The spies identify posts that are likely to undermine the authority of the government. Another type of censorship is the use of civil society to monitor social sites. This method was practiced in Tunisia.

The civil society in Tunisia monitored people who used technology to pass information in the country. Finally, the other type of censorship is media blackout. In this case, the interface of the social media website used by an individual does not appear.

Hence, the individual cannot perform any activity via the site when there is a media blackout.

Nevertheless, the internet has various implications on censorship of social media sites. Advances in technology make it difficult for governments of third world countries to censor the sites.

CHAPTER TWELVE

DOES PROTECTIVE DISCRIMINATION VIOLATE THE PRINCIPLES OF FAIRNESS?

The policy of giving favored treatment through protective discrimination's to certain members of the deprived groups because such groups have suffered systematic discrimination in the past has generated a fierce philosophical debate in the contemporary political theory. Such favored treatment include privileged access to jobs employment, admission in educational institutions, etc. and the recipients can be lower castes, classes, etc.

These politicize of protective discrimination's or rational discrimination's or affirmative action are also called reverse discrimination's because they embody race, class, caste or sex as the criteria for differential treatment just as overtly as it was used against them in the past.

While the egalitarian and positive liberals support such discrimination's in order to achieve adjust and fair society, the libertarians and legal positivists do not approve of such discrimination's because this, in their opinion, affects the excellence, merit and the basic rights of freedom and property of the individuals.

In the contemporary debates about equality, we do not talk of legal equality only in the sense of equality of opportunity but also 'equality of conditions' and 'equality of outcome or results'.

Since the son of a millionaire and the son of a laborer do not get equal opportunities, justice as fairness demands that the social environment must be changed if equal start for every one is to be provided. This can be achieved only through collective action. Also the 'equality before law' and 'equal protection of law' demand that everyone, should not be treated alike.

Though the legal equality has granted the equality of opportunity, but it has not been able to reduce economic and social inequalities whether based on race, sex, nationality, education, challenging the establishment of a just and fair society.

So the big question is how to bring about such an equality? One solution to this problem of creating an equalitarian and egalitarian society found in the twentieth century was to provide protective discrimination's that is giving unequal treatment to equals either by graphic favors or imposing a burden.

However, the policy of giving favored treatment through 'protective discrimination's' to certain members of the deprived groups because such groups have suffered systematic discrimination in the past has generated a fierce philosophical debate in the contemporary political theory.

Such favored treatment include 'privileged access to jobs, employment, admission in educational institutions etc., and the recipients can be lower castes, classes, women, children, tribals, negroes, backward classes etc'.

These policies of protective discrimination's or 'rational discrimination's' or 'affirmative action' are also called 'reverse discrimination's' because they embody race, class, caste or sex as the criteria for differential treatment just as overtly as it was used against them in the past.

While the egalitarians and positive, liberals support such discrimination's in order to achieve a just and fair society, the libertarians and legal positivists do not approve of such discrimination's because this, in their opinion, affects the excellence, merit and the basic rights of freedom and property of the individuals.

Protective Discrimination does not violate the principles of fairness

There are various justifications that the protective discrimination's do not violate the principle of fairness or justice. Some argue that protective discrimination's are examples of compensatory justice in order to rectify the past – wrongs of unjustified discrimination's against certain sections of the humanity such as lower castes, blacks, women, tribals etc.

Others appear to accept such prefertial treatment as necessary for end-state equality. There are others who are more pragmatic in the case of their race and wish to increase the number of their castes in the state administrator and other professions.

The legal aspect of equality emphasizes only equal opportunities which means that access to important social institutions should be open to all on universalistic grounds. This equality believes in merit.

That is, all occupational structures of society should be filled on the basis of merit and individual achievements and should not be based upon age, sex, wealth, religion etc. However, gradually it was found that the abstract equality of opportunity, though important, was not sufficient.

The concept of equality should also be viewed historically. Since everybody in the society does not start his life from the same line and a number of groups, classes, castes, tribals have been discriminated socially, economically, political, culturally, mere equality of opportunity would lead to accentuate further inequalities. Hence, equality of opportunity needs to be extended to equality of conditions.

In order to have equality of opportunity, it is essential to guarantee equality of conditions–i.e. all competitors in the race should start from the same point with appropriate handicaps. And the equality of conditions further requires equality of results or outcome.

It means that through legislation and political means, equality of results is achieved irrespective of starting point or natural ability. Social program of protective discrimination in favor of the disadvantaged groups such as scheduled castes, backward classes, tribals, blacks, children either through reservations or compensation are deemed fair in order to bring about a meaningful equality of opportunity for all.

There are various justifications that the protective discrimination's do not violate the principle of fairness or justice. Protective discrimination are based on this argument:

1. The equality of opportunity is very feeble.

2. It does not really exist unless made more effective.

3. There is a caused connection between being unequal and hence poor, illiterate, socially and culturally backward underfed and undernourished.

4. That something should be done to alter the distribution of goods and services in order to be fair to all.

5. Proactive discrimination is one of the various means to correct this imbalance in the distribution of good and services. As such it does not violate the principle of fairness.

Protective Discrimination violate the principles of fairness

Some scholars are of the opinion that the social philosophy behind protective discrimination's is somewhat confused and they have objected to it without dissenting from the ideal that social policy ought to take into account the injustice perpetuated on the lower classes.

The protective discrimination's are unfair in the procedural sense since granting privileges to individuals because of their birth, caste, race or sex is as discriminatory and unjust as denying them opportunity and jobs for the same reason.

It is also unjust since whatever wrongs were committed against their ancestors in the past, it is not clearly the case that today's young superior and meritorious individual - the victims of such preferential employment practices - are responsible for this. To demand a compensation for the wrongs committed by their forefathers is unfair.

The protective discrimination's violate the principle of fairness because they do not give consideration to merit and excellence. The libertarian are committed to developing the maximum level of excellence.

They argue that it is essential to maximize access and opportunity but that will not promote equality. In fact the emphasis should be more on mobility. The tendency cowards equality and distrust of excellence whether the educational institutions or employment is a great mistake.

Equality of opportunity is fine but if the education system tries to iron out distinction and merit, it is inexcusable. A society should try to foster the creation and preservation of what is best or as good as it possibly can be.

Such an aim can be pursued only by recognizing and exploiting the natural inequalities between persons, encouraging specialization and distinction of levels in education and accepting the variations in accomplishment in results. In fact the pursuit of excellence and creation of inequalities cannot be separated.

Such inequalities are inextricable from the recognition and pursuit of certain values too important to be compromised. The pursuit of excellence is also justified on the grounds that many original discoveries or creations eventually benefited everyone and others great works of architecture, for example, are important public goods.

Protective Discrimination and Social Justice under Article 15 and 16 of the Indian Constitution

Social justice means availability of equal social opportunities for the development of personality to all the people in the society, without any discrimination on the basis of caste, sex or race. No one should be deprived, because of these differences, those social conditions which are essential for social development. The issue of social justice is associated with social equality and social equality and social rights and these are depended on economic equality and rights. Social justice can be made available only in a social system where the exploitation of man by man is absent, and where privileges of the few are not built upon the miseries of the many.

The Preamble to the constitution of India assures to all citizens, justice - social, economic and political; Liberty of status and of opportunity and promotion among them all; Fraternity assuring the dignity and the unity of the nation. The spirit represented in the Preamble is further enshrined in the chapter of Fundamental Rights and Directive Principles of State Policy, the purpose of which is to promote the social welfare of the by securing and protecting as effectively as it may social order in which justice - social, economic and political shall inform to all the institution of national life. The 42nd Amendment Act by introducing the word "Socialist" in the preamble has strengthened the constitutional ethos of social and economies justice.

The constitution of India recognizes and seeks to realize the various components of social justice. Article 14 guarantees to every person "equality before law or equal protection of the laws within the territory of India". Article 15 (1) prohibits discrimination against any citizen on grounds of religion, race, caste and place of birth or any of them. In the same view Article 16 (1) provide equality of opportunity for all citizens in matters relating to employment or appointment to any office under the state. By Article 17 "untouchability" the age-old practice has been done away all its manifestations.

Article 15 (1) specifically bars the state from discriminating against any citizen of India on grounds only of religion, race, caste, sex, place of birth or any of them. Article 15 (2) prohibits subjection of a citizen to any disability, liability, restriction or condition on grounds only of religion, race, caste, sex or place of birth with regard to

(a) access to shops, public restaurants, hotels and places of entertainment.

(b) the use of wells, tanks, bathing ghats, roads and places of public resort maintained wholly or partly out of state funds or dedicated to the use of general public.

Under Art. 15 (3), the state is not prevented from making any special provision for women and children.

Art. 29 (2) does not prevent the state from making any special provisions for the advancement of any socially and educationally backward classes of citizens or for the Scheduled Castes and the Scheduled Tribes. Provisions contained in Arts. 15 and 16 arc merely enabling provisions. No citizen of India can claim reservation as a matter of right and accordingly no writ of mandamus can be issued. (a) Art. 15 (1) Article 15 (1) prohibits differentiation on certain grounds mentioned above.

Under Art. 15 (4), the State can make special provisions for certain sections of the society as stated above. But for any section of population not falling under Art. 15 (4), special provisions can be made if there is reasonable classification. The word 'discrimination' in Art. 15 (1) involves an element of unfavorable bias.

Art. 15 is narrower than that of Art. 14 in several respects. One, while Art. 14 is general in nature in the sense that it applies both to citizens as well as non-citizens, Art. 15 (1) covers only the Indian citizens and does not apply to non-citizens. No non-citizen can claim any right under Art. 15, though he can do so under Art. 14. Two, while Art. 14 permits any reasonable classification on the basis of any rational criterion, under Art. 15 (1), certain grounds mentioned therein can never form the basis of classification. The residents of Madhya Bharat were exempted from payment of a capitation fee for admission to the State medical college, while the non-residents were required to pay the same.

The Supreme Court negative the plea of discrimination by the non-residents under Art. 15 (1) because the ground of exemption was 'residence' and not 'place of birth'. Residence and place of birth are two distinct concepts with different connotations. Art. 15 (1) prohibits discrimination on the basis of place of birth but not residence. And, in the instant case, classification on the basis of 'residence' was held to be reasonable. Education is a State subject. A State spends money on the upkeep of educational institutions. There is, therefore, nothing wrong in the State if it so orders the educational system that some advantage ensures for the benefit of the State. Some of the resident students after securing their degree may settle in the State as doctors and serve the community. Thus, the justification for the classification on the basis of residence rested on the assumption that the residents of the State would after becoming doctors settle down and serve the needs of the people of the State.

Art. 15 (3) : Women and Children : Articles 15 (3) and 15 (4) constitute exceptions to Arts. 15 (1) and 15 (2).

According to Art. 15 (3), the state is not prevented from making any "special provision" for women and children. Articles 15 (1) and 15 (2) prevent the state from making any discriminatory law on the ground of gender alone. The Constitution is thus characterized by gender equality. The Constitution insists on equality of status and it negates gender bias. Nevertheless, by virtue of Art. 15 (3), the state is permitted, despite Art. 15 (1), to make any special provision for women, thus carving out a permissible departure from the rigours of Art. 15 (1). Articles 15 and 16 do not prohibit special treatment of women.

Socially and Educationally Backward Classes

A major difficulty raised by Art. 15 (4) is regarding the determination of who are 'socially and educationally backward classes.' This is not a simple matter as sociological and economic considerations come into play in evolving proper criteria for its determination. Art. 15 (4) lays down no criteria to designate 'backward classes', it leaves the matter to the state to specify backward classes, but the courts can go into the question whether the criteria used by the state for the purpose are relevant or not.

The question of defining backward classes has been considered by the Supreme Court in a number of cases. On the whole, the Supreme Court's approach has been that state resources are limited, protection to one group affects the constitutional rights of other citizens to demand equal opportunity and efficiency and public interest have to be maintained in public services because it is implicit in the very idea of reservation that a less meritorious person is being preferred to a more meritorious person. The Court also seeks to guard against the perpetuation of the caste system in India and the inclusion of advance classes within the term backward classes. From the several judicial pronouncements concerning the definition of backward classes, several propositions emerge. First, the backwardness envisaged by Art. 15 (4) is both social and educational and not either social or educational. This means that a class to be identified as backward should be both socially and educationally backward.

In Balaji case

The Court equated the "social and educational backwardness" to that of the "Scheduled Castes and Scheduled Tribes". The Court observed: "It was realised that in the Indian society there were other classes of citizens who were equally or may be somewhat less backward than the Scheduled Castes and Scheduled Tribes and it was thought that some special provision ought to be made even for them." Secondly, poverty alone cannot be the test of backwardness in India because by and large people are poor and therefore, large sections of population would fall under the backward category and thus the whole object of reservation would be frustrated.

Narayan Sharma v. Pankaj Kumar Lehkar

In Narayan Sharma v. Pankaj Kumar Lehkar, the Supreme Court considered the validity of the following scheme of reservation made by the Assam Government for seats in the post-graduate medical courses in its medical colleges:

(i) 25% All India quota,

(ii) 4 seats for North Eastern Council,

(iii) 6 seats for teachers in medical colleges,

(iv) 20 seats for doctors who had worked for five years in a health centre outside the municipal limits,

(v) 7% for Scheduled Caste candidates

and

(vi) 15% OBC candidates.

An entrance examination was to be conducted but candidates in categories (i), (ii), (iii) and (iv) were not required to appear at such an examination.

The Supreme Court upheld reservation for category (ii) as these seats were meant for the five Eastern States having no medical college of their own. The students of these States being handicapped in getting medical education formed a separate class and reserving a few seats for them did not violate Art. 14. But the provision exempting them from appearing at an entrance examination was quashed as selection ought to be based on merit and could not be left to the arbitrary discretion of any administrative body. Reservation for category (iii) was also upheld. It was mandatory for teachers in medical colleges to have a postgraduate degree for their future promotions. The classification was based on an intelligible differentia having rational nexus to the object of the rule. The teachers being constantly in touch with medical subjects could be validly exempted from the entrance examination.

Equality of Status and Opportunity in Public Employment

Article16 (1) is a facet of Art. 14. Arts. 14 and 16 (1) are closely interconnected. Art. 16 (1) takes its roots from Art. 14. Art. 16 (1) particularizes the generality of Art. 14 and identifies in a constitutional sense "equality of opportunity" in matters of employment under the state. An important point of distinction between Arts. 14 and 16 is that while Art. 14 applies to all persons, citizens as well as non-citizens, Art. 16 applies only to citizens and not to non-citizens. Article16 (1) guarantees equality of opportunity to all citizens "in matters relating to employment" or "appointment to any office" under the state.

According to Art. 16 (2), no citizen can be discriminated against, or be ineligible for any employment or office under the state, on the grounds only of religion, race, caste, sex, descent, place of birth or residence or any of them. Adherence to the rule of equality in public employment is a being feature of our constitution and the rule of law is its core, the Court cannot disable itself from making an order inconsistent with Articles 14 and 16 of the Constitution.

Article 16 (2) is also an elaboration of a facet of Art. 16 (1). These two clauses thus postulate the universality of Indian citizenship. As there is common citizenship, residence qualification is not required for service in any State. Public employment is a facet of right to equality envisaged under Article 16 of the Constitution of India. The State although is a model employer, its right to create posts and recruit people there for emanates from the statutes or statutory rules and/or rules framed under the proviso appended to Article 309 of the Constitution of India. The recruitment rules are to be framed with a view to give equal opportunity to all the citizens of India entitled for being considered for recruitment in the vacant posts.

Article 16 (1) is much wider in scope than Art. 16 (2) and the grounds of discrimination expressly mentioned in Art. 16 (2) are not exhaustive. Art. 16 (2) brings out emphatically, in a negative form, what is guaranteed affirmatively by Art. 16 (1). Discrimination is a double edged weapon; it would operate in favour of some persons but against some others. Art. 16 (2) prohibits discrimination and thus assures the effective enforcement of the Fundamental Right guaranteed in Art. 16 (1).

Educational qualifications can be made the basis for classification of employees in State service in the matter of pay scales, promotion, etc. Higher pay scale can be prescribed for employees possessing higher qualifications. Similarly, in the matter of promotion, classification on the basis of educational qualification so as to deny eligibility to a higher post to an employer possessing lesser qualifications is valid. Educational qualifications can justifiably be made the basis for qualification for the purpose of promotion to the higher post.

Articles 16 and 14 do not forbid the government from creating different cadres or categories of posts carrying different emoluments. Also, there is no bar in the way of the state integrating different cadres into one cadre. "It is entirely a matter for the state to decide whether to have several different cadres or one integrated cadre in its services. That is a matter of policy which does not attract the applicability of the equality clause."

The Supreme Court has deduced the principle of "equal pay for equal work" from Arts. 14, 16 and 39 (d) and the Preamble to the Constitution. No such principle is expressly embodied in the Constitution but the principle has now matured in a Fundamental Right.

State of Madhya Pradesh v. Pramod Bhartiya

As the Supreme Court has explained in State of Madhya Pradesh v. Pramod Bhartiya, the doctrine of "equal pay for equal work" is implicit in the doctrine of equality enshrined in Art. 14 and flows from it. The rule is as much a part of Art. 14 as it is of Art. 16 (1). The doctrine is also stated in Art. 39 (d), a directive principle, which ordains the State to direct its policy towards securing equal pay for equal work for both men and women.

Purshottam v. Union of India

In Purshottam v. Union of India, implementation of revised pay scales as recommended by the Pay Commission for certain categories of servants but non implementation there of for certain other categories was held to be discriminatory. The Government had made a reference to the Commission in respect of all its employees and when it accepted its recommendations, it should implement them in respect of all employees. Not to implement the recommendations with respect to some employees only violated Arts. 14 and 16.

Exceptions to Arts. 16 (1) and 16 (2):

The right of equality guaranteed by Arts. 16 (1) and (2) are subject to a few exceptions.

First, under Art. 16 (3), Parliament may make a law to prescribe a requirement as to residence within a State or Union Territory for eligibility to be appointed with respect to specified classes of appointments or posts. Thus, Art. 16 (2) which bans discrimination of citizens on the ground of 'residence' only in respect of any office or employment under the state can be qualified as regards residence and a 'residential qualification' imposed on the right of appointment in the State for specified appointments. This provision, therefore, introduces some flexibility and takes cognisance of the fact that there may be some very good reasons for restricting certain posts in a State for its residents.

Art. 16 (5) provides that a law may prescribe that the incumbent of an office in connection with the affairs of a religious or denominational institution or a member of the governing body thereof, shall belong to the particular religion or denomination.

Art. 16 (4) constitutes a very significant exception to the principle of equality embodied in Art. 16 (1) and, therefore, needs to be discussed in some detail.

In Balaji case, the Court attempted to impose a constitutional limit on the extent of preference, not on the "narrower ground of reservation," but on the broader grounds of policy. The Court spoke of adjusting the interests of the weaker sections of society with the interests of the community as a whole. The Court declared that a formula must be evolved which would strike a reasonable balance between the several relevant considerations.

While striking down as unconstitutional, a government order by which 68% of the seats in educational institutions were reserved for Scheduled Castes, Scheduled Tribes and Other Backward Classes on the ground of excessive reservation and as a fraud on the Constitution, the Court observed: "Speaking generally and in a broad way, a special provision should be less than 50 per cent, how much less than 50 per cent would depend upon the relevant prevailing circumstances in each case.

Immediately thereafter came the Devadasan case before the Supreme Court in which the Court was required to adjudge the validity of the 'carry forward' rule. The 'carry forward' rule envisaged that in a year, 17½ per cent posts were to be reserved for Scheduled Castes/Tribes, if all the reserved posts were not filled in a year for want of suitable candidates from those classes, then the shortfall was to be carried forward to the next year and added to the reserved quota for that year and this could be done for the next two years. The result of the rule was that in a year out of 45 vacancies in the cadre of section officers, 29 went to the reserved quota and only 16 posts were left for others. This meant reservation upto 65% in the third year and while candidates with low marks from the Scheduled Castes and Scheduled Tribes were appointed, candidates with higher marks from other classes were not taken.

CHAPTER THIRTEEN

SHOULD THE STATE INTERVENE IN THE INSTITUTION OF THE FAMILY?

The question of state interference in the family came into the forefront in the context of women liberation movement in Europe and America during 1960s and 70s popularly known as Feminism. A number of feminist scholars analyzed the subordinate position of women in the family and society and came to the conclusion that the gender difference was not neutral but an elaborate system of male domination which must be brought to an end. There has been a strong tradition that due to the biological differences, men are superior to women.

This gender difference is reflected vividly in the institution of Patriarchy. On a wider level, patriarchy is the manifestation and institutionalization of male dominance over women in the society. It is considered as a system of male authority which oppresses women through social, political and economic institutions. It is man's access to resources and rewards within and outside the home and family.

This power can be economic such as the right to be serviced, sexual such as marriage and motherhood, cultural such as devaluation of women's work and achievement, ideological such as representation of women as natural biological creatures inherently different from men. Historically this domination of men over women has been secured in a variety of ways such as:

Gender indoctrination,

Education deprivation,

The denial to women of knowledge of their own history,

By restraint and outright coercion,

By discrimination in access to economic resources and political power

and

By creating an overall ideology that women are inferior to men.

State Intervention in the Family is not Justified

All feminist theories believe that men and women experience the family in different ways. This is not ideological truism but is also a political and social fact. For centuries, marriage customs, conventions and laws have favored men rather than women. In-spite of legal reforms, the position has not changed substantially. However, there is sharp difference of opinion among the various schools of feminism about the role of the state in the institution of family. The liberal feminists limit the family to the 'private sphere', do not see the male oppression of women as a problem and want to keep the state away from the family.

With the changing view on the family during 1960's, the doctrine of family autonomy was challenged by many feminist writers. But this was defended once again by the liberal feminists by making a distinction between the 'public' and 'private' sphere and putting the family in the private realm. Classical liberals assumed that the male headed family is a biological determined unit. The natural equality they discussed was of fathers as representatives of families.

The contemporary theorist John Rawls says that the family is one of the social institutions to be evaluated by the theory of justice but for him the traditional family is just and goes on to measure just distributions in terms of the 'household income' which accrues to 'head of the Household' so that question of justice within the family is ruled out of court. The liberal feminism accepted the division between the public and private spheres and seeks primarily equality in the public realm. The family is excluded. The liberal feminists are committed to the public private spheres distinction and the see the family as the center of the private sphere.

Since the liberal right to privacy encompasses and protects the personal intimacies of the home, the family, marriage, motherhood, procreation and child rearing, hence, any proposal of interference in the family in the name of justice represents a clear departure from the traditional liberal conception of the family as the center of private life. In liberalism, domestic life falls outside both state.and civil society.

State Intervention in the Family is Justified

The radical feminists do not agree with the 'public' and 'private' distinction advanced by liberals. They explain the subordination of women in the family to the patriarchial organization in the society which is determined by a male hierarchical order that enjoys both economic and political power. This patriarchical system preserves itself through marriage and family. They believe that the marriage oppresses women and family breeds patriarchy. Family is a bastion of traditional values.

They consider family as a prison for women. It is at the center of both cultural devaluation and economic dependence of women. They believe that the fight for gender equality must go beyond public discrimination and should include domestic labor, women's devaluation of her work, her personal sphere and domestic life.

State Intervention in Family

The slogan of the radical feminists that 'the personal is political' and that 'women's body as women's right' claimed that the family is the root cause of women's oppression and it must be smashed. But this slogan has now given way to a new one: That the family, the so called personal sphere must be opened to political change, by force if necessary. The state should reach into the home to make it 'just'. Contemporary feminism poses a significant challenge to the liberal theory of family as the personal sphere and that the state should not interfere in the domestic scene.

In fact, the present state already intervenes in the family sphere by establishing the social background in which the family functions. But the radical feminists want the state to interfere directly in the family.

The traditional liberal concept views family as the center of private life, radical feminists such as Carole Pateman argue that the family and marriage contract are not private one at all and should not be treated as such. Family is one of the ways through which patriarchy sustains itself and the state must thrust justice into an inherently oppressive condition of marriage and family life. On the other hand, individualistic feminism demand that the state withdraw from family and allow the adults involved to work out their own definition of justice in the privacy of their own homes.

To the individualists, the state is already a partner in everyday family life. Marriage and divorce laws are made by the state. The state legally defines what is marriage and how it can be dissolved. Without government approval, no marriage can be terminated. The state has a controlling interest and the state must bear a great deal of the blame for the current evils of marriage and family.

Functions of Family

Some of the important functions of family are as follows:

Family is the most universal and fundamental social institution which performs a variety of functions in human society. Different sociologists have viewed or classified the functions of family into different types.

Famous Sociologists like Ogburn and Nimkoff have classified functions of family mainly into six types such as: (i) Affectional (ii) Economic functions (iii) Recreational functions (iv) Protective functions (v) Religious functions and (vi) Educational functions.

Another famous sociologist K. Davis have classified the functions of family into four main divisions such as (i) Reproduction (ii) Maintenance (iii) Placement and (iv) Socialization of the young. Davis calls these as social functions and opines that family also performs some individual functions which are a corollary of its social functions.

Similarly Goode classified the functions of family into five different types such as (i) Procreation functions (ii) Socio-economic security functions (iii) Status determination functions (iv) Socialization functions and (v) Social control functions.

Similarly Prof. Lundberg enumerated four basic functions of family such as (i) Regulations of sexual behavior of members and reproduction (ii) Care and training of children (iii) Co-operation and division of labor and (iv) Primary group satisfactions.

Similarly Reed classified functions of family into following four types such as (i) Race Perpetuation (ii) Satisfaction of sex needs (iii) Socialization and (iv) Economic functions.

But famous Sociologist Maclver classified the functions of family into two broad categories such as essential and non-essential functions.

These two functions are also widely known as primary and secondary functions.

Under essential or primary functions, MacIver includes mainly three functions such as (i) stable satisfaction of sex needs (ii) production and rearing of children and (iii) provision of a home.

Under non-essential or secondary functions he includes religious, recreational, educational, economic and health related functions. But one thing is clear that though sociologists have classified the functions of family into different forms still all of them gives stress on the same aspects in a different manner. However, these different functions of family are as described below:

(A) Essential functions of family:

MacIver has divided functions of family into essential and non-essential types. Under essential functions he includes mainly three functions such as, stable satisfaction of sex needs, production and rearing of children and a provision of home. But besides these MacIverian functions of family, family may also perform some other essential functions. But it must be remembered that essential functions are those functions which are basic or fundamental in nature and no other institutions can perform these functions so successfully as family can. However family performs the following essential functions:

(1) Stable satisfaction of Sexual needs:

This is the most important essential function of family. Family has been performing this functions since the inceptions of human civilization. It is a well known fact that sex urge is the most important and powerful instinct and natural urge of human being. It is the primary duty of family to satisfy the sexual urge of its members in a stable and desirable way.

Through the mechanism of marriage, family regulate the sexual behavior of its members. Because satisfaction of sex instinct brings the desire for life long partnership of husband and wife. Satisfaction of this sex needs in a desirable way helps in the normal development of personality. Ancient Hindu Philosopher Manu and Vatsayan opines that satisfaction of sex needs is the primary objective of family. If it is suppressed it creates personality maladjustments.

(2) Procreation and Rearing of Children:

It is another important sectional function of family. Necessary arrangement of stable satisfaction of sexual urge resulted in procreation. Family provides the legitimate basis for production of children. It institutionalizes the process of procreation. By performing this function of procreation family contributes to the continuity of family and ultimately human race. Hence perpetuation of human race or society is the most important function of family. Not only the production of children but also child rearing is another important function of family. Family is the only place where the function of child rearing is better performed.

It provides food, shelter, affection, protection and security to all its members. It plays a vital role in the process of socialization of child. It provides healthy atmosphere in which the personality of the child develops properly. Family takes care of the child at the time of need. Hence it is rightly remarked that family is an institution par excellence for the procreation and rearing of children. It has no parallels.

(3) Provision of Home:

Family perform another important function of providing a home for common living to all its members. It is only in a home that children are born and brought up. Even if children are born in hospitals in modern time still they are taken care of and properly nourished in a home only. Because family and a home have no substitute. In a home all the members of family live together and a child is brought up under the strict vigilance of all its members.

All the members need a home to live happily with comfort, peace and protection. A home provides emotional and psychological support to all its members. Man's necessity of love and human response got fulfilled here. Family provides recreation to its members. In a home family performs the role of a modern club. Man got peace by living in a home.

(4) Socialization:

It is another important essential function of family. It is said man is not born human but made human. New born human baby became human being after they are socialized. Family plays an important role in the socialization process.

It is one of the primary agents of socialization. Living in a family human baby learns norms, values, morals and ideals of society. He learns culture and acquires character through the process of socialization. His personality develops in the course of his living in family. From family he learns what is right and wrong and what is good or bad. Through socialization he became a social man and acquires good character.

(B) Non-essential or secondary functions of family:

Famous Sociologist MacIver has divided functions into essential and non-essential functions. Under non-essential or secondary functions he includes economic, religious, educational, health and recreational functions. Along with the essential functions family also performs these non-essential functions. These functions are non-essential or secondary in the sense that these are also performed simultaneously by other social institutions in family. These functions are as follows:

(1) Economic functions:

Since ancient times family has been performing several economic functions. It is an important economic unit. In ancient time family was both a production and consumption unit. It used to fulfill almost all the economic needs of its members such as food, clothing, housing etc. In the then days family was self-sufficient. But now a days almost all the economic functions of family is performed by other agencies and family only remain as a consumption unit. It do not produce anything. All the members of family now working outside the home.

But in spite of all family still performing some economic functions of purchasing, protecting and maintaining property. It also equally distribute property among its members.

(2) Educational functions:

Family performs many educational functions for its members. As an primary educational institution, family used to teach letters, knowledge, skill and trade secret to all its members. It looks after the primary education of its members and moulds their career and character. Mother act as the first and best teacher of a child. Besides he learns all sorts of informal education such as discipline, obedience, manners etc. from family. Of course at present many of the educational functions of family are taken over by school, college and universities sill family continues to play an important role in providing the first lessons and primary education to its members.

(3) Religious functions:

Family is the centre of all religious activities. All the family members offer their prayers together and observe different religious rites, rituals and practices jointly. All the members believe in a particular religion and observe religious ceremonies at home. Children learn different religious values from their parents. Living in a spiritual atmosphere spirituality develops among the children. Family transmits religious beliefs and practices from one generation to another. But at present family became more secular in their outlook. Common family worship became very rare and absolute. Still family continues to play an important role in shaping religious attitude of its members.

(4) Health related functions:

Family as a primary social group performs several health related functions for its members. It look after the health and vigor of its members. It takes care of the sick, old and aged persons of the family. By providing necessary nutritive food to its members family takes care of the health of all.

Of course modern family delegates some of its health related functions to hospital. The child is born today in a hospital or in a clinic and taken care of by nurses.

(5) Recreational function:

Family-performs several recreational functions for its members by entertaining them in various ways. In ancient period family was the only centre of recreation. All the members together organize family feasts, visit the family relations, organize family picnics, etc.

Family organize different festivals which is another source of recreation. The relationship between grandparents and grand children is another source of entertainment. After day's work all the members used to assemble and exchange their view. Of course modern club replaces many recreational functions of family. But at the same time it is said that present family acts as a modern club without its evil effects.

(6) Cultural functions:

Family also performs several cultural functions as well. It preserves different cultural traits. Man learns and acquires culture from family and transmits it to succeeding generations. That is why, family is considered as centre of culture.

(7) Social functions:

Family performs a number of social functions. It teaches about social customs, mores, traditions, norms and etiquette to the coming generations. Family exercises social control over its members and bring them into conformity with accepted standards. Senior members of family directly control the behavior of children and thereby they became a good citizen.

Functions of State

Some of the important functions of a state are as follows:

There is incessant controversy about what the state shall do. Political thinkers have from time to time advanced many theories to define the sphere of state activity. On the one hand, there are thinkers like anarchists, communists, syndic lists who question the very existence of the state and advocate a stateless society.

On the other hand, there are the absolute thinkers like idealists who regard the state omnipotent and entrust to it every action pertaining to human life. In between these two extreme types of thinking, there are the individualists who hold that Government is the best which governs the least. Thus, there is no unanimity among the political thinkers as to what the state should do.

The state is a limited agency:

The state has limits to what it can do. The state, as stated above, though universal yet it is a limited agency. It is limited by the means at its disposal. It is limited by the customs of the community.

It is limited by the fear of resistance. And it is limited by the existence of other associations in society whose function it cannot perform or undertake. MacIver says, "It is needless and futile to concentrate in one agency all the activities of life. Certain tasks the instrument can perform, but badly and clumsily — we do not sharpen our pencils with an axe. Other tasks it cannot perform at all and when it is directed upon them it only ruins the material."

From what MacIver says the conclusion may be drawn that there are certain functions which only the state can perform, others which it is wholly incapable of performing and those which it can with advantage perform and for which it is well adapted.

Maintenance of order:

Taking the first type of functions, i.e., which the state alone can perform, the primary function is the maintenance of order in society. The state is possessed of peculiar attributes which enable it to perform this function, it "has the power of life and death over all associations no less than over persons because of its unabated right to make war and peace."

It "claims the right to settle political disputes by force. In so doing it elevates political interests to complete supremacy over all other interests." It alone can make rules of universal application. "It alone can establish rights and obligations which admit of no exceptions. It alone can define the areas and limits of subordinate powers. It alone can co-ordinate within one great social framework the various organizations of a society. The state, in short is the guarantor and the guardian of the public order."

But order is not for its own sake, but "for the sake of protection and of conservation and development." It is justified only to the extent to which it serves the needs of the community in conformity with and limited by the ideals of the community, particularly by the ideals of justice and liberty.

For the maintenance of order, its primary task, the state performs a number of subsidiary functions like that of regulating and coordinating the work of other associations, defining the rights and obligations of citizenship, establishing and controlling means of communication and transportation, establishing units and standards of computation, measurement value etc., formulating specific rights and obligations of persons within the family, within the economic order and within other social relationships, maintaining armies and police and providing for justice.

Conservation and development:

Considering the second type of functions i.e., functions for which the state is well adapted, MacIver includes in this category "the conservation and development of human capacities as well as of economic resources." The state is well adapted to regulate the exploitation of natural resources in the interest of present and of future generations of the entire community.

If the exploitation of natural resources is left in the hands of private individuals, then they will seek their own gain at the cost of communal gain. The state can better uphold the interest of the whole and the interest of the future as against the competitive interests. So conservation of forests, fisheries and exploitation of mineral resources are functions which the state should undertake.

The conservation and development of human capacities are no less important than that of the natural resources. The state should provide for education, public parks, museums, playgrounds and contribute to the development of science and to the encouragement of art. Though other agencies can perform these tasks but none so efficiently and on so great a scale and with such authority as can the state.

It is thus clear that the modern state has expanded its activities in various directions. The ratio of the number of Government employees to the total population has steadily continued to increase. Whether the recent expansion of governmental activities is advantageous or not depends upon how one feels about the value of the increased functions and services and the cost of these functions and services.

On this question there may be strong difference of opinion. While the critics on the one hand point out to the evils of the growth of bureaucracy, the inevitable outcome of the expanding governmental activities, on the other hand, it is pointed out that the recent social and technological changes have made it necessary for the state to take over the functions formerly carried by other institutions.

We are living in an era characterized by the establishment of large centralized Governments which perform innumerable functions and exercise enormous powers. Perhaps it is not now possible to go back to the society of the small community. Accordingly, our problem is not to reduce the functions of the state or abolish it but to develop more adequate scientific knowledge and techniques for the efficient exercise of these powers in the public interest.

Should not control public opinion:

Taking up the functions which the State should not undertake, MacIver says, "The State should not seek to control public opinion, no matter what the opinion may be," provided there is "no incitement to break its laws or defy its authority." "To urge law breaking is to attack the fundamental order, the establishment of which is the first business of the state and for the preservation of which it is endowed with coercive power."

Should not enforce morality:

Secondly, the state should not enforce morality. The sphere of morality is distinct from the sphere of political law. "Morality is always individual and always in relation to the whole presented situation of which the political fact is never more that an aspect." There is no such thing as 'state morality'. There is no morality save individual morality. Law cannot prescribe morality, it can prescribe only external conditions. It cannot cover all the grounds of morality. "To turn all moral into legal obligations would be to destroy morality."

Should not interfere with custom and fashion:

Thirdly, the state should not interfere with custom and fashion directly. "The state has little power to make custom and perhaps less to destroy it, although indirectly it influences customs by changing the conditions out of which they spring." MacIver states in forceful words: "Custom, when attacked, attacks law in turn, attacks not only the particular law which opposes it, but, what is more vital, the spirit of law abidingness, the unity of the general will."

The state has even much less control over that minor and changeful form of custom called fashion. MacIver states, "A people will follow eagerly the dictates of fashion proclaimed by some unknown coterie in Paris or London or New York, but were the state to decree changes in themselves so insignificant, it would be regarded as monstrous tyranny, it might even lead to revolution."

Should not create culture:

Lastly, the state cannot create culture because culture is the expression of the spirit of a people or of an age. "It is the work of community, sustained by inner forces far more potent than political law." Art, literature and music do not come directly within the purview of the state. "In all these activities a people or a civilization goes its own way, responsive to the influences and conditions for the most part un-comprehended and uncontrolled by the state."

It may be emphasized here that in recent times there has been a tendency towards the growth of state functions. Today there is no citizen and almost no organization which operates outside its orbit of power. The barriers between the field of economics and government are rapidly being lowered. The welfare state is now a popular ideal. There is now hardly a phase of life in which the state does not participate either as a tenderer of services, as an arbiter, or as a controller.

The two world wars have further broadened the functions of the state. The trend towards expansion of governmental functions is likely to continue. This trend is the result of the growth and diffusion of the idea that the state is responsible for the economic and psychological, as well as the physical security of its citizens.

The conclusion to which MacIver is driven on the whole question of state action is that, in general terms the state should control those external conditions of social living which are of universal concern in view of the acknowledged objects of human desire. It should not meddle with concerns which are not its own. "If it attempts those things which it ought not to attempt it will fail in the things which properly fall within its charge."

The sphere of state action is undoubtedly vast still it is not omni-competent. It should refrain from the futile or pernicious effort to do those things which it is unqualified to do and gird itself more resolutely, more nobly to the fulfillment of those functions which it is well qualified to do.

www.ingramcontent.com/pod-product-compliance
Lightning Source LLC
Chambersburg PA
CBHW031539150726
47990CB00001B/227